WALKING IN ITALY'S
GRAN PARADISO

Martagon lily

WALKING IN ITALY'S
GRAN PARADISO

by
Gillian Price

CICERONE PRESS
MILNTHORPE, CUMBRIA

© Gillian Price 1997
ISBN 1 85284 231 8
A catalogue record for this book is available from the British Library

To Nicola, as usual, with all my love.

For tireless Bet & Dave, as well as Kathryn, Morgan and Giacomo who are just about big enough to carry their own rucksacks now.

Thanks to Nicola once more for his patient labour on the maps and diagrams, to Colleen for finding time to read the manuscript and offer helpful comments, to walking companions Bruno, Grazia, Piero, Edda & Gian Pietro, as well as all the ibex, chamois and marmots, too numerous to name individually, who make this area so special.

Photographs by
Gillian Price and Nicola Regine.

Cicerone books by the same author:
Walking in the Central Italian Alps
Walking in the Dolomites

Front cover: During the ascent to Rif.Deffeyes, with Lac du Glacier.
(Walk 32)

CONTENTS

Introduction

Walks

Appendices

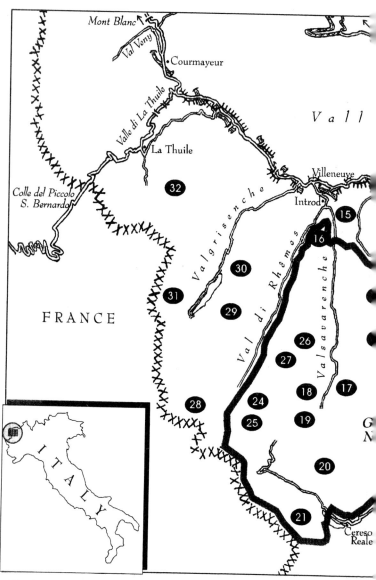

Mont Blanc

Val Veny

Courmayeur

V a l l

Valle di La Thuile

La Thuile

Villeneuve

Colle del Piccolo
S. Bernardo

32

Introd

15

16

Valgrisenche

Val di Rhêmes

Valsavarenche

FRANCE

30

29

31

26

27

18

17

28

24

25

19

G
N

20

ITALY

21

Cereso
Reale

8

Gran S. Bernardo

0 5 10 km

N

d ' A o s t a

Aosta

Nus

St.-Vincent

n d i C o g n e

Cogne

Valle di Champorcher

Hône-Bard

Ivrea

8

4

9

5

6

3

10

7

2

1

PARADISO NAL PARK

ITALY

23

Valle Soana

lle dell'Orco

Pont Canavese

Torino

lles

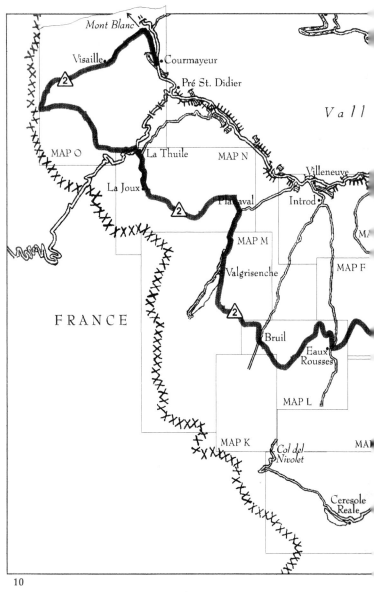

Mont Blanc
Visaille
②
Courmayeur
Pré St. Didier

MAP O
La Thuile
MAP N

Villeneuve

La Joux

②
Plan aval
Introd

MAP M

MA

Valgrisenche
MAP F

②

FRANCE
Bruil
Eaux
Rousses

MAP L

MAP K
Col del
Nivolet

MA

Ceresole
Reale

Vall

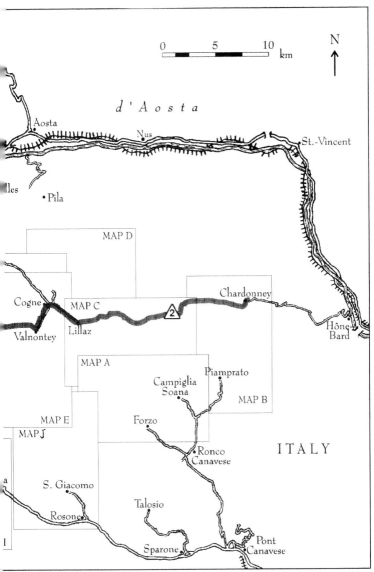

d'Aosta

Aosta
Nus
St.-Vincent

Pila

MAP D

Chardonney

Cogne
MAP C
Valnontey
Lillaz
Hône-Bard

MAP A

Campiglia
Soana
Piamprato
MAP B

MAP E
Forzo

MAP J
ITALY

Ronco
Canavese

S. Giacomo

Talosio

Rosone

Sparone
Pont
Canavese

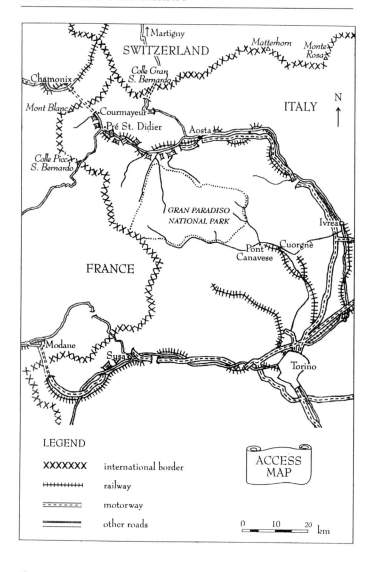

INTRODUCTION

THE GRAN PARADISO NATIONAL PARK

"Intending visitors to the district should be warned that when the King of Italy is hunting around Cogne (the present King has not been there since 1885) they may find their movements impeded by fear of disturbing the game. This will seem however but a small hindrance when set against the great facilities which the royal hunting paths (passable for horses) afford to travellers on the less interesting portions of many of the ascents in this group." This introduction appeared a little over one hundred years ago in *The Mountains of Cogne*, by alpine pioneers George Yeld and Rev. W.A.B. Coolidge, one of the first guides to be published on the area. In 1856 King Vittorio Emanuele II had unified several hunting reserves and declared a Royal Game Reserve. The move followed 1821 rulings that prohibited hunting in order to protect the ibex and chamois populations, at a worryingly low level. Ibex in particular had been hunted intensely since at least medieval times. It was considered a "walking pharmacy" as its blood, horns, bones and even droppings were employed in remedies for everything from poisoning to rheumatism. A special talisman was even made of the tiny cross-shaped bone found in its heart, believed to guard the wearer against violent death.

Not only did the ban on hunting - with the exclusion of royal entourages - encourage growth in both the ibex and chamois populations, it guaranteed their survival. Stock from these colonies has repopulated parks the entire length of the Alps.

In the mid 1800s some 350km of wide tracks were constructed at the King's expense, along with five hunting lodges and mountain huts, manned by a veritable army of gamekeepers (ex-poachers), beaters and porters.

After the First World War, however, in 1922, Vittorio Emanuele III, grandson of the "Hunter King", renounced his hunting rights and on his express wish had the area declared Italy's very first National Park, "for the purpose of protecting the fauna and flora, and preserving the special geological formations, as well as the beauty of the scenery".

The curious and romantic name Gran Paradiso goes back much further than the royal game reserves. While most experts say the name Gran Paradiso, referring to the 4061m peak, is a contortion of "Granta Parei", great wall, some accounts afford it a "heavenly" connotation in the context of the head of Valnontey with peaks named after San Pietro (St. Peter), San Andrea (St. Andrew), S. Orso (St. Ursus), without forgetting Punta dell'Inferno (hell) and Testa della Tribolazione (tribulation).

Geographically the area is part of the Graian Alps (the north part of the western Alps), possibly named after the mythical Greek hero Ercole Graio, alias Hercules, believed to have passed via Colle del Piccolo San Bernardo between labours.

Geologically speaking, the Gran Paradiso group started out over 230 million years ago as volcanic material, with a fraction of marine sediments. Tectonic activity led, in fits and starts, to the formation of the Alps during the Tertiary period (approx. 54-57 million years ago), the accompanying heat and pressure responsible for the transformation into metamorphic rock. The Gran Paradiso summit, for instance, is made up of a huge dome of augen-gneiss around which is a complex formation of calcareous and mica-schists, with characteristic areas of greenstone, to mention but a few. Of great economic significance to man have been the immense mineral deposits, notably the magnetite mined until recently at Cogne. Furthermore Valle dell'Orco, the main southern valley, owes its original name "Eva d'or" (water of gold) to the gold content of its sands. Copper, silver and gold mining were also widely practised, and visitors will often see abandoned mine sites during walks.

The area covered in this guide, the Gran Paradiso National Park and surrounding territory, straddles two regions of Italy - the Valle d'Aosta in the north and Piedmont (Piemonte) in the south. Though quite different now, the two regions shared long periods of history, and a brief overview must start from the prehistoric peoples, dating back to 8000 BC by some accounts. Later, a local Celtic population known as the Salassi was firmly established in Valle d'Aosta at the time of the arrival of the Romans, who routed them only after long opposition. The Roman city of Augusta Praetoria (Aosta) was founded in 25 BC, an important alpine junction on the Via delle

Gallie, many sections and bridges of which are still standing. It was alternately subject to Frankish and Burgundian rule. From the 11th century the entire area was controlled by the Savoys, becoming a Duchy in the Middle Ages. This continued virtually uninterrupted - except for a brief period under France with Napoleon's occupation and the transfer of sovereignty to the Kingdom of Sardinia - right up to 1861, with the Unification of Italy. Though French was the main language for most of the time, and is still taught and used, Italian is more widely used these days. Public signs are bilingual. Inhabitants on both northern and southern sides, however, speak an unusual patois of French-Provençal origin. This includes a wealth of specialised vocabulary for aspects of the natural alpine surroundings connected with the pastoral activities, as persists in place names.

Population-wise, the mid-1800s saw notable growth which put a strain on natural resources, leading to seasonal emigration. This involved itinerant tinkers, seed-sellers, chimney sweeps and glaziers from the southern valleys in particular. Later, however, large-scale emigration became permanent, and communities such as that in Paris have actually helped preserve the Valle Soana dialect. Contacts with the home village continue, and French numberplates are commonplace in village car parks during the holiday period. A 1981 census put the permanent human population of the Gran Paradiso at 8359, in sharp contrast to the 1881 peak of 20,616. This meant that a large number of villages were abandoned, and walkers will find themselves wandering along age-old paths punctuated with votive shrines and passing through long-empty hamlets decorated with intriguing religious frescoes, particularly in the southern section of the Park. In higher reaches the functionally designed shepherds' huts are an open book onto now historic lifestyles.

The Gran Paradiso National Park nowadays has a body of 68 rangers who spend their time carrying out essential wildlife censuses and discouraging poaching. Several Visitors' Centres are run by cooperatives in the summer months and include helpful if limited displays and collections of sad stuffed animals. They can be found at: Noasca (open year-round) and Ceresole Reale in Valle dell'Orco, Ronco Canavese in Valle Soana, Degioz in Valsavarenche, and Bruil in Val di Rhêmes (though it may be transferred to nearby Chavaney). Plans for a new centre at Cogne were also under way at the time of writing. Interesting guided walks are organised, though at the time of writing none is available in English, probably due to lack of demand. A yearly news sheet is also published, and English translations can occasionally be found at Tourist Offices or Visitors' Centres. The Head Office of the "Parco Nazionale del Gran Paradiso" is in Turin (via della Rocca 47, 10123 Torino, tel:011/8171187).

The Park does not have an easy life: poaching continues, storms frequently necessitate bridge and path maintenance work and funding has been cut drastically, meaning staff and facilities are forever insufficient. As is the norm for most Italian Parks, no entry fees are charged. Long-standing local opposition continues, because protected areas are often seen as "restrictive", allowing no internal development. Furthermore at peak times - summer Sundays and August - the few roads that lead into the Park see rivers of cars which disgorge hordes of day visitors. Col del Nivolet and the valleys around Cogne in particular are, understandably, favourite summer Sunday destinations for the inhabitants of north Italy's industrial cities as they flee scorching conditions in search of cool, breathable air. However the sheer volume of visitors has a negative and irreversible impact on the environment. Tourism is an essential activity for the local economy and the Park is an efficient magnet, but as in other protected areas a reasonable balance between freedom of access and environmental conservation must be found if the area is to have a future, as the Park authority is well aware. Alpine environments are not renewable resources.

Some statistics for the National Park: beginning with the royal donation of 2200 hectares, out of the present total surface area of 70,000 hectares (700sq.km) only 10% is wooded, 16.5% used for pasture and agriculture, 24% uncultivated, and 40% classified sterile. 9.5% is occupied by 57 glaciers which though of relatively reduced dimensions nowadays, nevertheless provide visitors (even those who are not equipped for actual ice traverses) with the chance to observe a fascinating series of ice-related phenomena: vast rock slabs polished smooth by the passage of some ancient glacier, groups of sizeable levigated rocks known as "roches moutonnées" due to their similarity with recumbent sheep, characteristic U-shaped valleys crafted by the long-gone ice mass, erratics or huge boulders carried afar by the glacier but of a recognisably different geological composition to its new neighbours. The telltale moraines, usually chaotic ridges of debris transported by the ice and deposited at its sides or front, are useful in determining the history of the area: bare moraine probably dates back to the last mini-ice age, a mere 1500-1800 years ago, whereas an average of 5000 years must pass before a ridge can be colonised by flora such as the "pioneer" Mountain Avens, after preparatory work by the likes of lichens. On the other hand trees such as larch or dwarf mountain pine need a little longer (15,000 years in all) before the soil is suitable for them to take root.

The glaciers themselves of course also mean abundant water from melting ice so the area is rich in water courses, spectacular waterfalls and an incredible string of lakes of all shapes and colours. This abundance of water, as well as meaning walkers never have far to look to quench their thirst (though drinkability is not always guaranteed), also attracted the hydroelectric dam builders who from the 1920s were virtually given free rein on the southern flanks, to provide Turin with the power its industries needed. This led to a considerable number of sizeable dams, conduits and power stations, accompanied by a series of maintenance staff buildings now in various stages of abandonment.

ACCESS & TRANSPORT

How to reach the area - see "access map" p12

The nearest airports in Italy are Turin (Torino) and Milan (Milano), though any of the northern airports can be used thanks to their proximity to the main Venice-Milan-Turin railway line.

From the north by public transport Valle d'Aosta can be approached by coach from France via Chamonix, or from Switzerland via Martigny. Otherwise from the south by train via Ivrea as far as Aosta or Pré-St.-Didier, only 5.5km before Courmayeur. Long-distance coaches also run from Turin and Milan.

The southern flanks of the Park are accessible via Turin, which in turn has international train connections via Modane in France. From Turin take the private train line as far as Pont Canavese.

Drivers have a greater choice of itineraries: from France via the Mont Blanc tunnel or the Piccolo San Bernardo Pass, whereas from Switzerland one uses the Gran San Bernardo Pass and tunnel. From

Pont Canavese - Turin train, at Cuorgnè station

the south as well as the main road, SSn.26, a motorway ("autostrada") leads via Ivrea to Aosta almost as far as Courmayeur. For the southern section you'll need SSn.460 from Turin via Cuorgnè hence Pont Canavese.

How to get around - internal public transport

North side - Valle d'Aosta:
Information on services from Aosta can be obtained from the central bus station ("Autostazione") across the road from the railway station. Summer bus timetables take effect any time between early June and July, ending early-mid September, depending on when the new school term starts. Variations from year to year are common, so it is essential to make enquiries on the spot.

The companies and valleys they serve are as follows:

BENVENUTO tel:0165/34507 - Valgrisenche
SAVDA tel:0165/262027 (Aosta) - Val di Rhêmes
SAVDA tel:0165/842031 (Courmayeur) - La Thuile, Val Veny
SVAP tel:0165/41125 - Cogne, Valsavarenche
VITA tel:0125/966546-7-8 - Champorcher
La Thuile Council c/o Tourist Office tel:0165/884179 - La Joux

South side - Piedmont valleys
The SATTI company is responsible for both the private railway line Turin-Pont Canavese, tel:0124/84279 (Pont), tel:011/5215523 (Turin), and the bus lines that connect the railhead (Pont Canavese) with the southern flanks of the Park, namely Valle dell'Orco and Valle Soana.

WHEN TO GO
The Park area and surroundings is of course open year-round, though access is subject to snow cover, avalanches and landslides which close roads and paths. The most suitable period for non-skiing visits ranges from May to October. The high altitude refuges usually operate July-September, but of course at other times you can make a base in any of the valley resorts.

May-June sees herds of ibex grazing on the fresh new grass on valley floors and even around roads and settlements, but by midsummer they have returned to their rocky spurs and are observable around the 2200m level, never far from chamois. Around September they all descend a little in search of food once more. For flower lovers, however, July is probably the best month.

August is peak holiday time for Italians, and valley accommodation is best booked in advance. The higher refuge-to-refuge itineraries are feasible then with less snow cover on the passes - crowds are rare in these high reaches at all times. Late summer brings crystal clear days, burnt autumn colours and deserted paths, whereas in October the odd snow spatter is not uncommon. Italy now stays on summer time until late October, meaning a bonus of extra daylight for visitors. The choice is yours.

LOCAL TRADITIONS
A brief note is in order to cover the kaleidoscope of cultural events the area offers. In addition to visits to the numerous castles in the main Valle d'Aosta, the most characteristic happenings are the unusual "Battailles des Reines". Probably traceable back to prehistoric times, they see two enormous pregnant cows engaged in (bloodless) battle, for the honour of being decorated "Queen". Each competitor has already established herself as best milker-cum-battler at the head of a herd. Emotional local tournaments involving

entire villages start in March, and the grand final is the Regional Championship held late October in Aosta. Copies of the "Calendrier des combats" (open to all) are available from tourist offices. The practice is also extended to goats with the "Bataille des Tzevres" held in Valgrisenche in September.

A series of enthusing age-old 'bat and ball' individual or team sports is still closely followed, so if you are interested keep an eye out for "fiolét", "rebatta", "palét" or "tsan".

Otherwise long processions to high altitude sanctuaries are a favourite midsummer activity. Popular local occurrences with a legendary or religious origin, they attract huge crowds, often emigrants who return punctually each year for the occasion. Worthy of mention are the Notre Dame des Neiges procession to Lago Miserin (August 5th), the mammoth San Besso celebrations at Campiglia Soana (August 19th), and "Lo Patron de Sen Grat" (September 5th), all dealt with in individual walks.

For further information the following regional tourist organisations can be contacted, as well as the local offices listed at the end of the walk descriptions.

For the southern valleys: Azienda di Promozione Turistica del Canavese, Corso Vercelli 1, Ivrea (TO), tel:0125/618195-618131.

For the Valle d'Aosta: Ufficio Turistico di Aosta, Piazza Chanoux 8, Aosta (AO), tel:0165/236627, as well as Comunità Montana Grand Paradis, Villeneuve (AO), tel:0165/95055.

WALKS & WALKING
The National Park alone offers 470km of prepared paths (a good few summers' worth of walking!), complete coverage of which is not claimed by this guide. Rather, the itineraries described here through some wonderful areas of the Park and surroundings will hopefully stimulate walking appetites. With a map and a sense of adventure, scores of other walks can be concocted. The long distance route Alta Via 2 has also been included in the Appendix.

A stroll across pasture or through a wood, a steep climb over rough unstable terrain or even a snow-ice traverse - the range of terrains is vast, and there are possibilities for all legs and lungs. An explanation of the level of difficulty is given in the brief preface to each walk, though adverse weather conditions or extra snow cover will add several degrees of difficulty.

Timing, based on an averagely fit walker, is given for each stage as well as for the total walk, however it *does not include* stops for rests or meals, so always allow for extra time. Roughly speaking it is based on 1h for 300m in ascent or 500m in descent, otherwise some 5km on level ground (though don't expect much of that commodity here). Profile diagrams accompany each walk so that the timing, height gains and losses and steepness involved can be seen at a glance, in preference to distance, of limited usefulness in alpine circumstances.

Path marking varies wildly, going from the classical Italian Alpine Club markings of red and white paint stripes with the number in black, to the yellow arrows and stripes, often accompanied by signposting, of the Valle d'Aosta's recent marking campaign. A further popular "variant" involves faded or nonexistent marks, hence guesswork for walkers. Then there are the lifesavers called cairns, appropriately referred to in Italian as "ometti", little men. These mounds of stones heaped up by thoughtful walkers seem banal, but on an uncertain path in low cloud they stand out like beacons, while painted marks are swallowed up by the mist. Details of the type of waymarking to be expected on each walk are always provided in the descriptions, though of course conditions are subject to change, hopefully for the better.

The majority of the walks are traverses or circular itineraries, and alternative accesses or exits are given where feasible. Timing for the reverse direction is also given in brackets at the end of each stage. Furthermore smaller chunks can easily be bitten off at will.

Some important do's and dont's
Try and find time for some basic physical preparation prior to setting out on a walking holiday, as a reasonable state of fitness will make your excursions more enjoyable, not to mention safer.

Read walk descriptions before setting out and start gradually, choosing walks suited to your experience and state of fitness.

It is inadvisable to set out on a long route if the weather is uncertain. Areas such as those featuring extensive ice and snow fields can be unexpectedly submerged in a thick layer of mist, making orientation problematic. Rain, wind and of course snow are tiring and can make even easy paths dangerous. Ask at Tourist Offices or refuges for weather forecasts, or check the local newspapers. An altimeter is a useful instrument - when a known altitude (such as that of the refuge) goes up, this means the atmospheric pressure has dropped and the weather could change for the worse.

Always carry extra protective clothing as well as energy foods for emergency situations. Remember that the temperature drops an average of 6°C for every 1000m you climb.

In electrical storms, don't shelter under trees or rock overhangs and keep away from metallic fixtures.

The international rescue signals can come in handy: the call for help is SIX visual (such as waving a handkerchief or flashing a torch) or audible (whistling or shouting) signals per minute, to be repeated after a one-minute pause. The answer is THREE visual or audible signals per minute, to be repeated after a one-minute pause. Anyone who sees or hears such a call for help must contact the nearest refuge, police station or the like as quickly as possible.

The general emergency telephone number in Italy is 113. However calls for "soccorso alpino" (mountain rescue) can be made 24 hours a day to tel:0165/238222 in Valle d'Aosta, and tel:118 in Piedmont. Furthermore on the southern side the following villages have local contact numbers for mountain rescue: Ceresole Reale tel:0124/953188, Noasca tel:0124/901003 and Valprato Soana tel:0124/812933.

The following arm signals could be useful for communicating with a helicopter:

* help needed
* land here
* YES (to pilot's question)

* help not needed
* do not land here
* NO (to pilot's question)

Please don't stray from the path during excursions, especially not to shortcut corners as this can damage vegetation and cause erosion.

Rubbish-wise, carrying it all back down to the valley where it can be disposed of correctly means saving Park and refuge staff time and money. Furthermore, please don't leave unsightly paper lying around after a toilet stop.

Wildlife should not be disturbed unnecessarily or handled, tempting though it may be, especially for photographs. Under no circumstances are dogs allowed in the Park, even on a leash. Collecting flowers, insects or minerals is forbidden, as are fires and free camping.

MAPS

An excellent general road map is the 1:200,000 "Piemonte e Valle d'Aosta" map put out by the Touring Club Italiano and widely available in North Italy.

As far as walking maps go, the situation is dismal. Several publishers do suitable scale maps, but quite frankly they are riddled with errors and little effort is made to correct and update them. Path numbering rarely corresponds with the map (apart from the Alta Via routes), though this is due in part to the new waymarking system being introduced at the time of writing on the Valle d'Aosta side. Despite all their shortcomings, however, these walking maps are essential, and are all on sale throughout the area in bookshops and newspaper kiosks.

As the area covered by the guide is relatively compact, a single map is sufficient. The 1:50,000 walking maps which cover the National Park area and reach west as far as La Thuile are the N.3 "Il Parco Nazionale del Gran Paradiso" by IGC (Istituto Geografico Centrale, Turin), "Gran Paradiso" by Studio FMB Bologna (probably the most recommendable) and N.86 "Gran Paradiso-Valle d'Aosta" by Kompass (excluding several walks in the SE sector).

IGC has also put out several newer (but not necessarily updated) 1:25,000 versions, namely N.101 "Gran Paradiso-La Grivola-Cogne" and N.102 "Valsavarenche-Val di Rhêmes-Valgrisenche". For the final westernmost stage of the Alta Via 2, you'll also need IGC sheet n.4 or the FMB "Monte Bianco".

The maps included in this guide aim to give an idea of the location of the routes described together with significant geographical features, but are not intended as substitutes for the commercial maps listed above. Limitations of space and colour have meant the exclusion of paths other than those described, together with water courses unfortunately. Where several versions of a place name exist, the locally used one has been preferred, otherwise spelling follows the IGC 1:50,000 map usage.

The following is an explanation of the symbols used on the maps included in this guide:

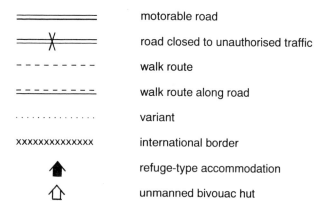

═══════	motorable road
═══╳═══	road closed to unauthorised traffic
– – – – – – –	walk route
─ ─ ─ ─ ─ ─	walk route along road
. . . .	variant
xxxxxxxxxxxxxx	international border
▲	refuge-type accommodation
⌂	unmanned bivouac hut

ACCOMMODATION

Everything from luxury hotels through to high altitude guest houses, converted farms, cosy refuges, spartan sanctuaries and metallic bivouac huts is available, not to mention camping grounds. As far as hotels go, several low key establishments are listed at the end of relevant walk descriptions, however a comprehensive brochure, updated yearly, is available for both the Valle d'Aosta and Piedmont valleys. Similar booklets are available from tourist offices for camping grounds and mountain refuges.

1) Refuges

"Rifugi" are mountain huts usually located in marvellous high altitude spots, and which provide hot meals and overnight accommodation during the summer. Many were constructed by branches of the Italian Alpine Club as well as local families, and come in various shapes and sizes - a converted hunting lodge, ex-electricity board building, old farms and the like. As well as providing attractive destinations in themselves, the beauty of the network of refuges is the flexibility it gives walkers and climbers. The atmosphere is friendly and helpful and the staff means a motley crew including students, assorted members of local families and alpine guides. They share all tasks including unloading the precious supplies brought in by helicopter, jeep, mechanised cableway, horseback or even backpack. Due to the strict regulations, only refuges outside the Park boundaries can make use of the mechanised means, hence the last two manual methods.

The refuges referred to in this guide are run by private families as well as the Italian Alpine Club CAI (Club Alpino Italiano), and anyone is welcome to stay. There is usually the choice between a bunk bed in the dormitory ("dormitorio"), where blankets or continental quilt are provided though a personal sleeping sheet is a good idea, or a room with fresh linen. In the CAI refuges, members enjoy discounted rates as do those of Alpine Clubs with reciprocal agreements (the long list includes clubs and associations from Australia, Austria, Canada, China, Denmark, Finland, France, Germany, Great Britain, Greece, India, Ireland, Israel, Japan, Korea, The Netherlands, New Zealand, Norway, South Africa, Spain, Sweden, Switzerland and the USA). "Mezza pensione" or half board (meaning dinner, bed and breakfast) is commonly offered and while not compulsory, is usually a good deal. Remember to change enough foreign currency before setting out on walks as refuge staff cannot be expected to accept anything but Italian lire in cash.

Mod cons such as hot showers (or even a bathroom if it comes to that) are few and far between, and the water may not always be suitable for drinking purposes - "acqua non potabile". This is not necessarily due to harmful bacteria, but could mean either a lack of mineral salts if the water comes from a glacier, or a low temperature (Italian law puts the minimum temperature for drinkable water at 14°C). While a small amount will not necessarily be harmful, stomach cramps and diarrhoea can result. If in doubt stick to safe bottled mineral water, on sale everywhere.

Food-wise these huts all guarantee hot meals at both lunch and dinner, and you have the choice of a pasta dish or "minestrone" vegetable soup, followed by second courses of meat and various side dishes. Regional culinary specialities may be on offer, and among those worth trying are "polenta concia", a delicious and filling thick corn meal porridge mixed with cheese; delicate "carbonata", meat stewed in red wine with spices; "risotto alla valdostana", a rice dish with melted cheese, not to mention special local cheeses such as fontina and toma. An interesting if limited array of wines comes from the few vineyards in the Valle d'Aosta, usually supplemented by the fuller bodied (and less costly) Piedmont wines such as Barbera. Stronger stuff comes in the form of aromatic "Genepì", known for its digestive properties and made from the flowers of the same name (and not to be confused with juniper). The "grolla", a decorated covered wooden bowl with multiple mouthpieces, may appear after dinner - filled with a mixture of coffee, red wine, grappa (wine spirit), sugar and lemon. It is passed around for measured sips, hence its name the "cup of friendship".

Relevant refuges (but only those with accommodation) and guesthouses are listed at the end of each walk description, along with their sleeping capacity and opening period. These dates (in brackets) will vary from year to year, depending on local conditions, so if in doubt, especially at the start or close of the season, do check by phoning the refuge itself where possible or asking at the nearest Tourist Office. Bookings (by phone) are only really necessary on July-August weekends, and will only be held until 6pm. Should you change your route, do notify the refuge to cancel as rescue operations (at your expense) might be set in motion when you don't show up. Refuge guests should always sign the register and indicate their next destination (or hotel guests tell the staff their planned route for the day) as it could help point rescuers in the right direction in a search.

A couple of final notes: "lights out" is 10pm-6am when the refuge generator is turned off, though breakfast may be served pre-dawn if the hut serves as a base for an important ascent. Walking boots, together with bulky ice and mountaineering gear, should be left on appropriate racks in the hallway, and slippers are often provided. Smoking is not allowed unless there is a separate room.

As well as the main premises, refuges usually have a "ricovero invernale", literally a "winter shelter". Adjoining the main building, they are spartan but always open, according to CAI regulations. Intended primarily for emergency use when the refuge is closed, they could also be used by walkers out of season. Intending users, however, must be fully equipped with sleeping bag, food, stove, utensils and so on. All the refuges listed in this guide have a "ricovero invernale" with the exception of two huts on the southern side of the Park, namely Rif. Jervis and Rif. Casa Alpinisti Chivassesi (both cited in Walk 21).

The "Rifugio" designation is often used in this area for a sizeable building, though not necessarily manned. So you will find huts referred to as "rifugio", always open as per a bivouac hut and with basic facilities, but only actually staffed for a brief period at peak times. The only cases in this guide are Rif. Miserin (Walk 4) and Rif. Pocchiola-Meneghello (Walk 23). They are shown as refuges on the map.

2) Bivouac huts
A "bivacco" can be the classic mountaineer type, a rounded metal container (with basic bunk beds and blankets) or at the best a converted shepherd's hut with running water, wood or gas stove and blankets. They are not always left open, thanks to inconsiderate users in the past. Information on where to collect the key etc. can be found under the relevant walk.

There is not usually any charge to use them, though there were rumours at the time of writing about CAI plans to introduce a minimum fee (5000 lire), payable at a local post office, to go towards maintenance costs.

You will also come across a series of modest huts (38 in all) marked on maps as Casotto or Capanna PNGP (Park hut). They belong to the Park for use by rangers or visiting experts, and are available to walkers exclusively in emergency situations.

3) Posto Tappa
The "Posto Tappa", the Italian version of the French "gîte d'étape", is a building that has been adapted to provide basic accommodation

for walkers, usually in a village. Several are cited for the southern valleys and they were set up for walkers on the long-distance route GTA - Grande Traversata degli Alpi.

They essentially mean hostel-like accommodation, sometimes with the use of a kitchen, otherwise a restaurant in the proximity serves low price meals on agreement. Charges are similar to those in refuges.

4) Camping
Free camping is forbidden within the National Park itself, but there are grounds with excellent facilities in most valleys, as follows:

Vallon di Cogne:
> Les Salasses (Lillaz) tel:0165/74252 (open year-round)
> Al Sole (Lillaz) tel:0165/74237 (year-round)
> Vallée de Cogne (Fabrique near Cogne) tel:0165/74079 (year-round)
> Bouva (Valnontey) tel:0165/74181 (1/7-30/9)
> Lo Stambecco (Valnontey) tel:0165/74152 (1/6-20/9)
> Gran Paradiso (Valnontey) tel:0165/74105 (20/5-30/9)

Valsavarenche:
> Pont-Breuil (Pont) tel:0165/95458 (1/6-30/9)
> Gran Paradiso (Plan de la Presse, near Pont) tel:0165/95433 (15/6-15/9)
> Grivola (Bien) tel:0165/905743 (15/6-7/9)

Val di Rhêmes:
> Marmotta (Rhêmes-Notre-Dame) tel:0165/906118 (15/6-15/9)
> Val di Rhêmes (Rhêmes-Saint-Georges) tel:0165/907648 (1/6-10/9)

Valle dell'Orco:
> L'Usignolo (Noasca) tel:0124/901026 (summer)
> La Peschiera (San Meinerio, near Ceresole Reale) tel:0124/953222 (summer)
> Piccolo Paradiso (Foiere, near Ceresole Reale) tel:0124/953235 (1/5-30/10)
> Villa (Villa, near Ceresole Reale) tel:0124/953232 (1/4-30/10)

Valle de la Thuile
> Rutor (Sapinière) tel:0165/884165 (year-round)

Val Veny

    La Sorgente (Plan Peuterey) tel:0165/89372 (1/6-30/9)
    Aiguille Noire tel:0165/869713 (20/6-15/9)
    Val Veny-Cuignon tel:0165/869073 (1/7-15/9)

EQUIPMENT
A few suggestions:

    * Sturdy walking boots with nonslip Vibram-type sole, preferably already worn in.
    * Light footwear for evenings.
    * Suitable clothing to deal with everything from scorching sun to a snow storm.
    * Lightweight sleeping sheet - on sale in many CAI refuges.
    * Gaiters.
    * Rain gear.
    * Sunglasses, sun barrier cream, hat and chapstick. (Remember that for every 1000m you climb the intensity of the sun's UV rays increases by 10%. This, combined with lower levels of humidity and pollution which usually act as filters, and possible snow cover which reflects a good part of the UV rays, make it essential you use a cream with a much higher protection factor than you would at sea level.
    * Altimeter, compass and binoculars.
    * Torch.
    * Mineral salts are extremely useful to combat salt depletion caused by excessive sweating in hot weather, and manifest in undue weariness and symptoms similar to heat stroke. (Isostar or similar)
    * First aid kit (with plenty of band aids).
    * Water bottle (the plastic bottles mineral water is sold in are perfect).

FAUNA
One of the main reasons for visiting the Gran Paradiso is the marvellous opportunity for observing wildlife at close quarters. It may seem superfluous to say so, but the best way to see the animals is actually to look out for them, as they are perfectly camouflaged amidst their surroundings. Desolate rock-strewn cirques might

Ibex at rest below the Gran Paradiso, Valsavarenche

reveal fawn patches which on closer inspection turn out to be chamois, levellish grassy ground is pitted with entrances to marmot burrows, and abandoned farm buildings overgrown with nettles may host vipers. Uninviting rock crests are worth perusing with binoculars for the likelihood of ibex sentinels actually tracking the progress of walkers. The formidable ibex, is of course, the recognised King of the Gran Paradiso. Previously known as "bouquetin" or "Steinbock", this stocky wild goat is easily recognisable from a distance for its enormous backward-curving ribbed horns, which can grow up to a metre in length on males. Well established and protected these days, they now number a record 5300, in contrast to the 300 reported by Yeld and Coolidge in 1893, and the 400 survivors after the Second World War. For ibex-viewing, the immediate surroundings of Rif. Sella in Valnontey are guaranteed. There on a typical summer's evening the young males will attract your attention with their clashing horns as they engage in mock battle silhouetted on high ridges. Meanwhile sedate older males graze unperturbed, ignoring onlookers, some distance from small herds of timid females with their young. High rocky terrain acts as a stage for their unbelievable acrobatic displays, but herds shift around in search of

Very young marmot

grass and can even be seen on valley floors during the winter.

The chamois, on the other hand, can also be seen in woods as well as the high rocky outcrops. Another type of mountain goat, it is slender and daintier than the ibex, with shorter hooked horns, not to mention white patches on its face and rear. A recent count put its numbers at 7700. Principal predators are the fox and eagle, but long snowy winters take an even greater toll on the population, and this applies to the ibex as well.

It's hard not to at least hear a marmot with its shrill whistle warning of imminent danger, if not actually see a well-padded rear scampering over grassy hillocks towards its burrow. These comical beaver-like vegetarians live in large underground colonies and 8-10,000 were reported at the last census. Protected now, they were once hunted for their fat, used in ointment form as a cure for rheumatism.

Probably the easiest way to see a red fox is to wait outside a refuge at nightfall, as the scavengers come for titbits in the rubbish.

A sizeable carnivore returning gradually westward through the Alps is the mysterious lynx. Sightings of the tufted-ear feline with grey-brown mottled fur have already been reported by hunters and rangers in Valle d'Aosta, where it prefers the shelter of low altitude woods, the habitat of its favourite prey, roe deer, though evidently it does not disdain old ibex slower on their feet when afflicted with conjunctivitis.

Another recent arrival is the wild boar. Not a native to the area, it was introduced to populate several low altitude hunting reserves and has bred so successfully that it is becoming a nuisance, wreaking havoc in the chestnut woods.

A noteworthy amphibian is the common frog, renowned for its ability to spend winters frozen into ponds up to altitudes of 2500m, thawing back to life with the arrival of spring. In the reptile line, on dry southern hillsides around 1500m the bright emerald sheen of the green lizard is hard to miss, while several varieties of snake are occasionally glimpsed, usually sunning themselves on paths or old stone walls. The most common is the poisonous and protected asp viper (no relation at all to the Egyptian cobra!). This greyish-brown snake has a clear diamond pattern along its back and is slightly smaller than the common viper found in Great Britain. It is always featured on the helpful posters in tourist offices, visitors' centres and refuges. Extremely timid, it only attacks when threatened, so do give it time to slither away should you encounter one on the path. (Elementary precautions walkers can take are to keep their legs covered when traversing an overgrown zone, and tread heavily. Should someone be bitten, keep calm and seek medical help as soon as possible. Bandaging and immobilisation of the limb are usually recommended in the meantime. Remember that you do have about 30 hours' "leeway", and moreover, if there is no swelling after 2 hours have passed, it either means that no venom entered the blood stream or it wasn't a viper at all.)

Higher up glide ubiquitous flocks of chaotic noisy orange-beaked crows, more correctly known as alpine choughs. Their only equals in noise are the raucous European jays, which flash blue feathers on their dashes through the mixed woods lower down. Impressive ample shadows may be cast by golden eagles, who have a field day in spring and summer preying on young marmots and lambs, the scarcity of vegetation facilitating their hunt. The only competition in terms of territory comes from the largest bird in the Alps, the lammergeier or bearded vulture. Not a hunter itself it

Santuario di San Besso - Walk 2
At Finestra di Champorcher looking down Vallon de Urtier, with the
point of the Grivola in the background (right) - Walk 4

prefers carcasses. It is able to swallow bones up to 30cm in length (digestion then requiring 24 hours!), and is renowned for its ability in cracking bones by dropping them from a great height in order to get to the marrow. With a maximum wing span of 3m, its wedge-shaped tail distinguishes it from the eagle, whose tail is rounded when seen from below.

Re-introductions of birds born in captivity took off in 1986 in Austria then spread to other parts of the Alps (1994 saw the first actual release in Italy), and sightings are now a frequent occurrence. Otherwise an impressive stuffed specimen is on display at the Bruil (Val di Rhêmes) Park Visitors' Centre.

Other fascinating spectacles are offered by clouds of butterflies which vie for supremacy in brightness - notably the metallic hues of the common blue "Icarus" butterfly. Then perching on a thistle is the rare Red Apollo, pale grey-cream but with trademark black and red "eyes" on its wings.

Last but not least, a mention is due to the so-called glacier flea, large numbers of which form widespread dark patches on the surface of glaciers and snow fields up to 3800m. The 1-2mm creature is hairy or scaly and mottled brown, feeding on organic matter such as pollen carried up by the wind. Red-tinted snow on the other hand could either mean sand from a far-off desert, incredible though it may seem, otherwise a cold-loving alga which contains a blood-red colouring. And that effectively introduces the realm of plants.

FLORA
An excellent place to begin a look at the remarkable array of alpine plants is the Giardino Botanico Alpino "Paradisia" in Valnontey. An incredible 1500 alpine species flourish there during summer (see Walk 11 for details), and a good 250 are found wild in the Park.

The relatively limited woods in the Park are composed mainly of mixed conifer, dominated by larch and Arolla pine on the upper edge, along with juniper shrubs. Common are curious dwarf versions of trees such as the net-leaved willow and ice-age relict dwarf birch. The range of flowers starts with the record-holding glacier crowfoot, which grows up to 4200m, to move on to colonisors of screes and

The upper waterfall at Lillaz (Walk 5)

33

Alpine Pasque flower

bare rock, such as saxifrage whose roots penetrate cracks and manage to fragment the stone. Moving downwards a little, stunning carpets of white ranunculus and Pasque flowers cover high pasture basins such as the Piano del Nivolet. Marsh land is often punctuated with soft white cotton grass and the tiny carnivorous butterworts, blue-violet (common variety) or yellow-white (alpine). Larch woods share their habitat with alpenrose shrubs and their pretty pink blooms, as well as wine-red martagon lilies and the minute flowers produced by bilberry and cowberry plants, in preparation for their late-summer fruit. The famous edelweiss is relatively unusual, as is the calcareous terrain it requires, but another ice-age relict, the rare twinflower, grows in several valleys.

This alpine environment is extremely hostile to life in general, and a season for high altitude flora can be as short as 60-70 days, including growth and reproduction. Each species has of course developed survival techniques ranging from thick hairy layers as protection from the cold wind and evaporation, as well as ground-hugging forms that minimise exposure, allow the plant to exploit the heat from the earth, and ensure protective snow cover, to mention a few. In addition to the beating they get from the elements, many also risk being nibbled by chamois (especially attracted to large-flowered leopard's-bane for its sugar content) and marmots (who seem to go for forget-me-nots), and even thoughtless picking by humans.

To end on a "spiritual" note, a quick mention is in order for the insignificant-looking but strongly aromatic male flower of the yellow genipi, found on stony grassland. Though it is rather rare and protected, local inhabitants are permitted to gather a limited number to prepare their beloved "Genepì", a perfect after-dinner drink with guaranteed digestive properties to boot.

A recommended companion for flower-lovers is *Alpine Flowers of Britain and Europe* by C. Grey-Wilson & M. Blamey (Harper Collins, 1995).

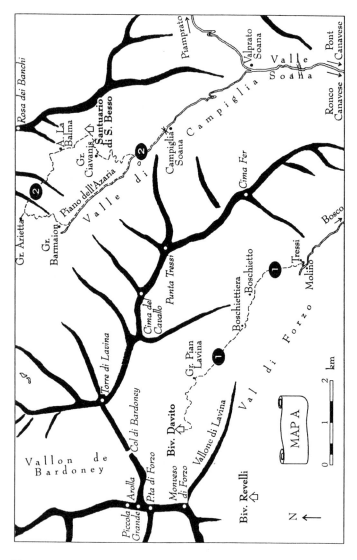

Val di Forzo - Frescoes and Fridges

via Tressi - Boschiettiera (1h10min) - Biv. Davito (2h30min) - Tressi (2h20min)
Total walking time: **6h (1-2 days suggested)**

Added to the National Park in 1979, quiet Val di Forzo branches off Valle Soana to run in a northwesterly direction. Its northernmost fork culminates in a vast wild rock-strewn cirque, in the shade of little-known 3300m giants Monveso di Forzo, Punta di Forzo and elegant Torre di Lavina. While the walk has Biv. Davito and its desolate setting as its destination, the fascinating first stage uses an old paved access path to the now abandoned hamlet of Boschiettiera, well worth a visit for a glimpse of the past world of medium altitude alpine life. En route are rock niches housing colourful frescoed votive shrines dating back to the 1700s, possibly the work of itinerant artists as a certain similarity in style can be observed in the historic religious frescoes throughout these southern valleys.

While the walk is rather lengthy, there is plenty of variety and the good condition of the path makes it suitable for all capabilities. **A sole note of warning:** in low cloud or mist, a somewhat common phenomenon in these high valleys, orientation becomes difficult in the upper valley above the tree line.

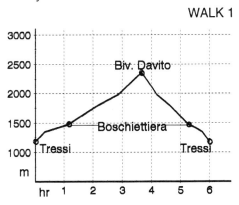

WALK 1

Rock shrine in Val di Forzo

As far as Biv. Davito goes, the tiny (basic) metallic hut stands in a particularly isolated position, making an overnight stay there a special experience.

No accommodation is available in Tressi or the nearby hamlets of Molino (bar only) or Forzo, making Ronco Canavese the closest useful centre (shops, hotel).

Note: the other major arm of Val di Forzo separates off at the village of Forzo to run westward. While not described in detail here it is good walking territory. Another unmanned hut, Biv. Revelli, is to be found in its upper reaches at 2610m, some 4h by signed path (n.605) from Forzo.

Access: by car you can drive all the way to the start of the walk. By public transport, however, the Val di Forzo turn-off (at Bosco, 1km before Ronco Canavese) is the closest bus stop on the year-round Pont Canavese-Valprato Soana line (SATTI company). The 5km walk up the asphalt road via Molino to Tressi is not unpleasant and the locals are not adverse to hitchhikers. 280m in gradual ascent is involved, so allow 1h15min on foot.

Stage One: ascent from Tressi to Boschiettiera (1h10min)
On the final curves of the road above the village of Molino, marked path n.608 forks off left, just before Tressi (1185m) is actually reached. It detours the hamlet and bearing left (N), crosses a dry torrent bed. The old path (frequent red waymarking) proceeds clearly between low stone walls through abandoned orchards and meadows. An easy climb through hazel trees brings you onto a rocky rise on the right-hand bank of impetuous Torrente Forzo opposite old stone houses. Steps cut out of the rock lead to an exceptional example of religious folk art, a wayside votive shrine under an impressive rock overhang. *Dating back to 1748, it was restored in 1867 then 1992, hence the bright colours of its multitudinous saints.*

A side stream is crossed, and the path continues climbing as the valley narrows. Next to a rustic bridge n.610 turns up right through swaths of yellow broom to the hamlet of Boschietto, visible on a rise with its white church tower (a worthwhile detour, time permitting). N.608 continues W alongside the ice-blue torrent and traverses meadows with ash and sycamore trees to the once-thriving settlement of Boschiettiera (1486m). Nowadays it boasts but several summertime residents, drinking water and a communal oven (still said to be in working order), not to mention more intriguing votive frescoes.

(Path n.604 crosses the torrent and heads W to Biv. Revelli in the neighbouring branch of Val di Forzo.)

Stage Two: to Biv. Davito (2h30min)
This upper section of Val di Forzo is called Vallone di Lavina. Keep on up the right-hand side of the torrent, NW now. Steeper stretches pass through larch wood with plenty of wild berries.

As the gradient levels out somewhat among the last larch trees, the valley opens out with a lovely vision of a broad rock platform, legacy of some ancient glacier, and beyond which is a light grey semicircular ridge. Torre di Lavina is N, and despite its name, is more like a pyramid than a tower. After crossing a small stream via boulders, several abandoned huts are encountered on a rise (Gr. Pian Lavina, 1796m), a second group huddling beneath a rock overhang a little further up. Consider yourself halfway at this point.

The path bears left across another dry watercourse, and steps cut into the rock climb in a zigzag through spreads of alpenrose and green alder shrubs. A pasture clearing is studded with an amazing concentration of black vanilla orchids, while a signboard reminds you these are the realms of the National Park.

Yet another stream is crossed beneath a small waterfall, and you wind up to more old stone huts, Alpe Costa (1979m), where a rest will give you time to admire views SE down the valley. *The grazing cows in the vicinity are brought up for the summer pastures, but the shepherd is rarely in residence, preferring the comfort of his village.*

The landscape becomes more desolate with every step you take and the path is not always clear, though cairns and red paint splashes suffice. There is a further group of huts (Gr. Lavinetta, 2092m) in a lovely basin run through with rivulets, which make for marshy terrain (and wet feet). *Several curious huts here are low, turf-roofed affairs, and rather than providing dwellings for alpine dwarves, once served as low energy, cool storage of dairy products - primitive precursors of the refrigerator.*

You continue up past a collapsed hut, directly above which a sizeable cairn is visible (actually on the edge of the platform where the bivouac hut is located). The path, clearer now, heads leftish below it, with a final wide swing right to come out onto the rock platform where you eventually reach yellow-painted Biv. Davito (2360m).

Experienced walkers (only) can proceed NW for the remaining 500m in ascent, to 2833m Col di Bardoney (allow 1h30min). *The pass had a bad reputation in the past for the unusual number of fatal accidents that overtook the Val Soana coppersmiths travelling north in search of work, despite a well-used mule track, now totally disappeared.* From the pass it is possible to descend into Vallon de Bardoney (see Walk 6), and continue to Lillaz and Cogne. The itinerary is however very long and there are no possibilities of accommodation before Lillaz.

Stage Three: descent to Tressi (2h20min)
As per the ascent route.

BIV. P.M. DAVITO, CAI, sleeps 4 (always open). Contains several well-used blankets and pillows, but no cooking gear. Water from nearby stream.

BIV. RAVELLI, CAI, sleeps 6 (always open)
ALBERGO CENTRALE (Ronco Canavese) tel:0124/817401
TOURIST OFFICE RONCO CANAVESE tel:0124/817401-817377
(seasonal)

WALK 2 *(see map A, p.36)*

Valle di Campiglia - The San Besso Cult

**via Campiglia Soana - Santuario di San Besso (2h) - Alpe La Balma
(20min) - Grange Arietta (1h25min) - Grange Barmaion (1h) -
Campiglia Soana (45min)**
Total walking time: **5h30min (1 day suggested)**

An engrossing combination of ancient legend and Christian beliefs,
centred on an early martyr and possibly the area's first evangelist,
Besso, comes into play here. A Roman soldier in the Thebean legion,
he escaped persecution in Martigny in the 3rd century AD and took
refuge in the upper reaches of Valle Soana. However after a period
spent successfully converting the local shepherds, he was hunted
out and unceremoniously thrown off the high rock overhang (M.
Fauterio) beneath which the sanctuary stands today. Not long
afterwards, on December 1st (which then became the saint's day)
shepherds recovered the body by digging where blood stains
appeared on the snow.

For meteorological reasons however, celebrations, are held
unfailingly on August 10th, attended by the faithful and hangers-on
in long processions. After the celebratory mass the weighty statue
of the saint, dressed as a Roman centurion, is carried around the
sanctuary by bearers who vie with each other for the honour, which
may mean by offering the largest sum of money. At the head is the
scarlet-robed priest bearing the relics of the saint.

In addition a curious habit is associated with the sanctuary, that
of souveniring fragments of greenstone as a lucky charm, as it is
believed to have miraculous properties. Scholars have linked this to
both ancient pagan cult practices as well as San Besso himself, well-
known for his powers of healing.

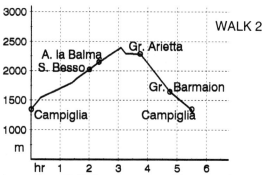

Participants from Valle Soana are joined by many from Cogne to the north, consolidating age-old links and traditions. Cogne, like Champorcher, was first settled from these southernmost valleys, and the inhabitants used to return regularly via the Valle di Campiglia carrying their dead for burial as they had no priest, as well as products for sale at the market of Cuorgnè (near Pont Canavese), where a special area was reserved for them.

Apart from the rewarding complete loop walk described here, including a panoramic traverse (with the occasional crumbly exposed stretch), the ascent as far as the sanctuary is a worthwhile excursion in its own right. Marmots and a wealth of wild flowers are guaranteed, while those who venture higher up will be rewarded by the sight of chamois. As relatively low altitudes are involved, the walk is usually feasible as early as June and as late as October, depending on snow falls.

As regards accommodation, in addition to the modest bivouac hut (Ricovero Bausano) at the Sanctuary, true to tradition as the erstwhile site of a royal hunting lodge, Campiglia Soana offers but a 4-star hotel complex (no single night accommodation). Nearby Valprato has a modest guesthouse ("locanda").

Note: Campiglia has no shops, so buy picnic supplies at Valprato.
Access: Campiglia can be reached on the SATTI company summer bus extension (mid-June to mid-September) from Valprato Soana, 2.5km downhill, where the service terminates at other times. The line originates at Pont Canavese (train connections with Turin).

There are plenty of parking areas for drivers.

Stage One: ascent to Santuario di San Besso (2h)

From the bus stop near the WW1 cenotaph at Campiglia Soana (1350m), follow the road uphill NW past the hotel and car park. At a short distance it is unsurfaced and closed to unauthorised traffic, and a wooden bridge crosses to the right-hand side of Torrente Campiglia. As the watercourse cascades away left, you continue steadily upwards to the clear turn-off right, marked for San Besso (20min this far).

Path n.625 climbs N through light mixed wood with elder and raspberry shrubs, while the open mountainside is thick with the blooms of the martagon lily and purple orchids, around which flutter colourful butterflies. A passage diagonal left climbs past a rock outcrop and up to an old hut (approx. 1800m), with a good view NW to the upper valley.

The path veers left (N) to enter the side valley with simple summer farm Grangia Ciavanis (1876m) and its cloud of flies, not far from a lovely waterfall. The Sanctuary buildings are visible now NE, in the shelter of a pointed rock overhang (M. Fauterio), on the lower reaches of Rosa dei Banchi. The way up the steep flank twists and turns, slippery underfoot at times due to the presence of greenstone, which is abundant here. *The rock, basic in geological terms, also means terrain suitable for purple alpine asters, pink thrift, and felted edelweiss, which brighten the meadows above the sanctuary, perfect for picnic purposes.*

Adjoining the Santuario di San Besso (2019m) is the Ricovero Bausano bivouac hut, but basic emergency shelter is always possible in one of the numerous huts here. *The church itself is locked, but the statue of San Besso, alias Roman centurion, can be made out inside.*

(Allow about 1h30min in the opposite direction.)

Stage Two: traverse via Alpe La Balma (20min) then 2400m saddle (45min) to Grange Arietta (40min)

Signposted path n.625 skirts beneath the church and bivouac building, to head NW across pasture dotted with lovely wild flowers. Several side streams are crossed, but keep to the right-hand side of the main watercourse, Rio S. Besso, for the time being. However, from the cluster of huts, Alpe La Balma (2152m), go sharp left down across the (probably dry) stream bed. A dirt path soon becomes evident climbing a ridge westish (several cairns) towards a depression. (Ignore the occasional red and white waymarking left, and stick to the path.) The southernmost flanks are carpeted with alpenrose, and chamois are often visible. From the first saddle aim for the low depression straight ahead. (Don't be tempted by the cairns that lead up right - the route for Colle della Balma.)

From the 2400m saddle the Valle di Campiglia opens up dizzily at your feet, and there are views W towards its head and Torre di Lavina SW.

The narrow but clear path bears right now, WNW for the most part. The traverse consists essentially of alternating ups and downs, with several stretches where the rubble-earth mixture has given way. It is a little slippery when wet, necessitating extra care. *The unstable nature of the terrain is due to the succession of several geological strata consisting of different rock types.* After some 40min coasting along the southern flank of the Rosa dei Banchi, the shepherds' huts of Grange Arietta (2288m) in their pasture basin are reached. (Total 1h30min for the reverse direction.)

A path continues NW to 2939m Col d'Arietta, the connecting pass for Cogne and the age-old route used by its inhabitants. The original path has reportedly all but disappeared in the immediate vicinity of the pass, and the crossing is for experienced walkers.

Stage Three: descent via Grange Barmaion (1h) then Piano dell'Azaria to Campiglia Soana (45min)

Go back briefly along the path you arrived on, then turn down right on n.624. It drops to cross a stream near a waterfall. Larch trees start gradually, and the path winds down (SSW), steeply at times, in their meagre shade. As the valley floor is approached, keep to the left of the farm buildings (Grange Barmaion, 1651m) without crossing the watercourse again, to reach the vehicle access track. Once one of the king's game routes, it runs SE along the delightful Piano dell'Azaria. *This quiet ample valley has several modest dairy farms, and at the time of writing there was talk of establishing an alpine botanical garden here.* The return walk is a pleasant stroll on the left bank of the wide torrent. Some 30min down the San Besso turn-off is passed, then it's over the bridge and down to Campiglia Soana where the walk started out from.

(Some 2h20min are necessary in the opposite direction.)

RICOVERO BAUSANO (SANTUARIO DI SAN BESSO) Private, sleeps 10. Keys from Signor Besso (sic) Vezzetti tel:0124/812936 (Via Roma 3, Valprato Soana). 5000 lire charged per person. Blankets, wood stove (good idea to collect fuel on way up) and running water available.

LOCANDA ALPINA (Valprato Soana) tel:0124/812929. Sleeps 8

DOMAINE GRAN PARADIS (Campiglia Soana) tel:0128/812886-812882. Sleeps 140

TOURIST OFFICE RONCO CANAVESE tel:0124/817401-817377 (seasonal)

WALK 3 *(see map B, p.46)*

Valle Soana/Valle di Champorcher - Spirits En Route to Col Larissa

---

via Piamprato - Col Larissa (3h) - Rif. Dondena (1h15min) - Creton (40min) - Chardonney (1h20min)
Total walking time: **6h15min (2 days suggested)**

An interesting walk in itself, especially for the wide-ranging outlook from Col Larissa, the itinerary is useful for transferring from the southern Valle Soana to the Valle di Champorcher. It was in fact long used by the locals for this purpose, not to mention the king's hunting parties on the 19th century game track constructed through the pass. Long paved stretches have survived and help render it trouble-free for today's walkers.

Wild flower enthusiasts will be delighted by the vast range encountered, especially on the approaches both sides of the pass. Midsummer is recommended on this account.

To enable the walk to be shortened (to 5h) for a single-day traverse, a variant exit is given during the descent. It leads directly to Chardonney, though can be further shortened by taking the Laris cable car.

As far as accommodation on the southern side is concerned, the most convenient hotel is at Valprato Soana, whereas Piamprato

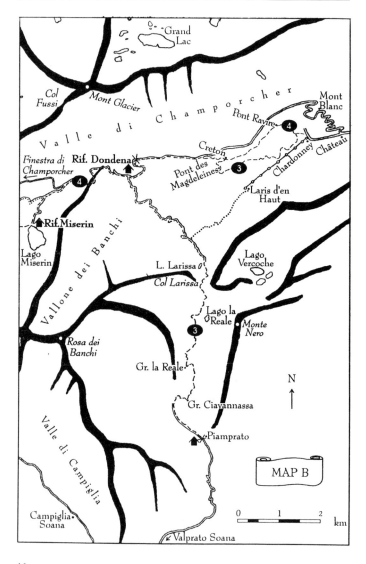

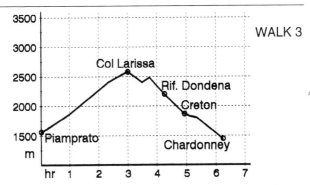

boasts a "Posto Tappa GTA", namely the old and tiny school house converted into a refuge where walkers can overnight for a modest fee.

Access: A SATTI bus from Pont Canavese ventures up the ever-narrowing road to the starting point of Piamprato (mid-June to mid-September). At other times it terminates at Valprato Soana, some 438m in altitude and 5.7km below.

The finishing point, Chardonney has year-round bus connections (VITA company) down to the railway station at Hône-Bard (in Valle d'Aosta).

Parking is possible at both Piamprato and Chardonney, but unless you do a short return walk, a car is a hindrance here as it would virtually take a full day to return via public transport to collect it.

Stage One: ascent via Grangia La Reale (1h40min) to Col Larissa (1h20min)

Nowadays hardly anyone stays on through winter at the village of Piamprato - recent reports in fact put the number at five. The large church and numerous old stone buildings dating back to the 1700s are indicators of a past long-term and more sizeable community. Chronicles from the 1600s recount a devastating avalanche that completely swept away the sizeable village.

From the parking area and bus stop at Piamprato (1551m), head N straight through the village, with an eye out for the tiny old school on the left (Posto Tappa GTA). *A 19th century plaque on its wall expresses gratitude to the king.*

Take the wide (authorised vehicles only) dirt road n.630 N alongside the torrent. Pass old farm buildings, several wide bends (not worth shortcutting) and the road ends (40min). As the 1993 flood washed away a section of the original path here, it's more straightforward at this point to follow the newer path up right. You make your way up dark grassy banks (red and white waymarking reappears from time to time) to the low farm buildings belonging to Gr. Ciavannassa (1865m, about 1h this far). *Latecomers might glimpse the bats from the retinue of a past resident, a terrible witch.* Climb up behind the first building to the higher constructions. From here the regularly marked path keeps leftish (but ignore the fork towards the torrent despite the direction given by most maps) above the water course, climbing in zigzags (due N).

It emerges onto a lovely flat basin brightened by pink alpenrose shrubs, and heads briefly left (W) across the torrent and up to an old-style summer sheep farm Grangia La Reale (2095m). *The King of Sardinia evidently had a lead mine in the vicinity, hence the denomination "reale", royal.*

You soon enter the domain of the National Park, and as though to confirm the fact that the area is under special protection, masses of pink hairy primroses carpet the slopes.

The path climbs easily through a series of upper valleys, and the pass (Col Larissa) can soon be identified to the left of a pylon.

The mountain over right (N), Monte Nero, was another scene of evil doing. *A devil once tricked the villagers of Piamprato into gathering below it to await the Madonna, who in fact appeared just in time to stop the rocks crashing onto the onlookers, as per the dreadful original plan.*

At about 2400m (some 40min before the pass) the path turns right to cross the torrent. Cairns point up to where vestiges of the royal game track are obvious above picturesque Lago La Reale (2412m). It leads across grass studded with lilac round-leaved penny-cress then rubble, with white glacier crowfoot blooms. A long diagonal stretch completes the ascent to Col Larissa (2584m).

In clear conditions the spectacular views from this ample saddle range from the triangle of Rosa dei Banchi and its small glacier WSW, then the first line of mountains to the N, including Monte Avic towering over its lake, further behind which, with any luck, the Matterhorn and Monte Rosa will be visible. Views S even take in Monviso and the Maritime Alps.

(Just over 2h should suffice in the opposite direction.)

Stage Two: descent to Rif. Dondena (1h15min)

You are not likely to meet many other walkers on this stretch.

Over predominantly greenstone, follow the yellow and black triangle waymarking of Alta Via 4 downhill. Snow usually lies late here but the wide game track is soon clear. A small lake is passed (Lago Larissa, 2486m) but the most striking feature of this area is the vivacity of spreads of flowers. *You're dazzled by the tiny blue jewelled clumps of gentians, large bright violets, a variety of saxifrages, as well as the insignificant-looking but aromatic yellow genipì, used for flavouring a local drinkable spirit.*

After about 30min a small watercourse is crossed (approx. 2400m), and an alternative exit is possible:

Alternative exit via Lares (45min) to Chardonney (45min)
At this point an unnumbered but clear path turns off right (NW) across the grass slopes and drops to join other paths for Laris d'en haut (1940m) and the cable car (Sundays only June to mid-September, as well as daily mid-July to end August). On foot instead from here head N towards the old royal game track below Creton (see Stage Three).

From the watercourse the track climbs gradually to the top of a ski lift (2480m), above the fertile Dondena pasture basin and the refuge. *Edelweiss and thrift flower on the calcareous terrain here.* Views include Mont Glacier (NW) and even far-off Monte Rosa (NE).

The track winds down W into the Vallone dei Banchi, the torrent consisting of meltwater from the glacier beneath Rosa dei Banchi, SW now. At an old stone hut (2300m) shortcut down to the bridge. Then as the path heads right (N), AV4 turns off left (towards Lago Miserin), whereas you soon reach Rif. Dondena (2200m). *The hospitality and cuisine (such as roasts accompanied by local polenta and mushrooms) make up for the rather bare concrete building, a converted royal hunting lodge, surprisingly enough.*

(Reverse timing - some 2h30min.)

This is a good place to slot into the traverse W to Cogne (see Walk 4).

Stage Three: descent via Creton (40min) to Chardonney (1h20min)
Leave the refuge down the wide dirt road that leads past old
barracks and through pasture to the torrent crossing and Dondena
parking area (15min). Further down the road the yellow and black
triangles for Alta Via 2 point down right via the original royal game
track, and passes through the hamlet of Creton (1873m). Heading
southish, you wind down to the Torrente Ayasse and across two
wooden bridges (Pont des Magdeleines), then past a ski lift. The
path immerses itself in a shady mixed wood, including masses of
wild roses and alpenrose beneath larch and green alder. The torrent
in the meantime is crashing its way through a narrow neck. Further
on path n.5 from Laris and the cable car arrives.

Red-eyed Apollo butterflies abound in a clearing with old huts
and a cross, then it's back into the final stretch of wood, with delicate
laburnum blossoms. Tight curves lead below the cable car and a
further farm, then finally across the torrent once more and into
Chardonney (1448m, shops and accommodation).

The bus stop is at the large parking area near the cable car
station.

(In ascent this stage requires 2h30min.)

For further details on this valley, see Walk 4.

LOCANDA ALPINA (Valprato Soana) tel:0124/812929. Sleeps 8
RIF. DONDENA tel:0125/37206 Private, sleeps 24 (30/6-30/9)
POSTO TAPPA GTA (Piamprato) C/O tel:0124/812926. Sleeps 8
(1/6-15/9). Shower and kitchen provided, plus specially priced
meals at a nearby restaurant
TOURIST OFFICE CHAMPORCHER tel:0125/37134
TOURIST OFFICE RONCO CANAVESE tel:0124/817401-817377
(seasonal)

WALK 4 *(see maps B & C, pp.46 & 52)*

Valle di Champorcher/Vallon di Cogne - Our Lady of the Snows and Power Lines

---

via Chardonney - Rif. Dondena (2h30min) - Rif. Miserin (1h30min) - Finestra di Champorcher (1h) - Lillaz (3h30min)
Total walking time: **8h30min (2 days suggested)**

This is quite a walk both in terms of historical associations and distance, following a very old route east-west via the Finestra di Champorcher pass thus linking the Valle di Champorcher with the Vallon di Cogne and the northern edge of the National Park. Frequented by witches, medieval travellers, religious processions, transhumance groups, royal hunting parties, it was used more recently for the incongruous passage of the "Superphenix" power lines from the French nuclear power plant in the Isère, not to mention the long-distance route Alta Via 2.

As far as the starting point goes, the inhabitants are descendents of herdsmen-settlers of the southern Valle Soana. There are at least two picturesque explanations for the name Champorcher: the first concerns San Porciero, a Roman legionary and companion of San Besso (see Walk 2) said to have taken refuge in 302 AD near Lago Miserin, where he started preaching; a second explanation attributes it to the pigs (swine) once bred in the valley on the nuts of oak and beech - these once prolific trees died out in the wake of a 16th-17th century drop in temperature.

The Miserin lake and sanctuary-cum-refuge is the site of an important local procession held religiously every August 5th in honour of "Notre Dame des Neiges" (Our Lady of the Snows). The cult originated late 4th century after an unexpected (August 5th!) snowfall in Rome. Participants from the neighbouring valleys of Cogne and Valle Soana join the locals in a celebration of their historic ties.

On the whole the area is quiet and lacks the crowds of the central National Park valleys, while still hosting sizeable herds of ibex and

51

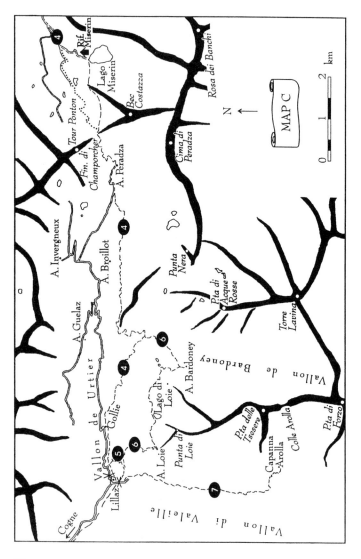

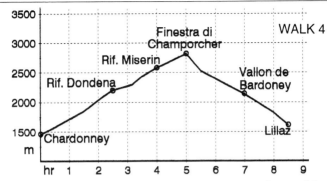

chamois, not to mention the ubiquitous marmots. One striking feature of this itinerary is the stunning mass of wild flowers, particularly in upper Vallon de Urtier (the higher part of Vallon di Cogne), best early to mid summer. An unusual combination of calcium-rich mica-schists produced by the metamorphism of clay sediments alternated with calcareous layers is responsible for providing the favourable soil conditions.

The walk itself is straightforward, if long, and often follows the wide riding tracks, heritage of the king's hunting days.

One of the many worthwhile 1-day loop walks the Champorcher valley offers, starts at Dondena (drive this far - see *ACCESS*) and proceeds via Rif. Dondena, Lago Miserin (on variant path n.7), around via Finestra di Champorcher, with a direct return to Dondena. The complete circuit needs about 5h in all.

Walkers starting out here on the Alta Via 2 should follow the route via Creton to Rif. Dondena (see Walk 3, Stage Three), slightly different from the ascent described here in Stage One.

The starting point Chardonney (its name a reference to "agglomeration of thistles") has several small hotels and shops. Here you can stock up on "sargnun" a tasty cheese (object of the "fêta d'i sargnun", village festival held late September) which comes fresh, salted or smoked, to be eaten with "pane nero", the local rye-bread, rock hard as per tradition (baked but twice a year!) which led to the invention of those wooden bread boards with a built-in chopper you'll see on display here.

Access: Coaches and slow Ivrea-Aosta trains stop at Hône-Bard in

Valle d'Aosta. From the small square near the railway station (in the shadow of the extensive 11th-18th century fortress) are year-round buses W the 16km up the Valle di Champorcher to Chardonney (VITA company).

Private vehicle access is possible as far as the parking area at Dondena (2100m, 20min on foot before Rif. Dondena): 1.5km before Chardonney (at Château, Champorcher) a road turns up N and its narrow curves are asphalted as far as the hamlet of Mont Blanc. A decent if unsurfaced road continues the remaining 5km, but drivers are warned that they proceed at their own risk on this stretch. (At several points along this road are entry paths into the recently instituted Parco Naturale del Monte Avic to the N.)

At the end of the walk, Lillaz, the first inhabited village you reach in the Vallon di Cogne, is served by (SVAP company) bus from Cogne (July to mid-September only). Otherwise it takes some 45min on foot for the 3.5km.

Stage One: ascent from Chardonney via Creton (1h30min) to Rif. Dondena (1h)

From Chardonney (1454m) and its cable car, head uphill to the bridge left across the torrent (AV2 signposting). Not far up is a junction where you take n.9 right (leaving the old hunting track). The delightful old path proceeds upwards NNW through pine wood to a bridge (Pont Ravire, 1567m) across the cascading Torrent Ayasse. The path is true to the name of the locality, known as "La Scaletta" (or Echelette), little staircase, continuing its steep climb (SW) on a series of rock slab steps.

Once past the hamlet of Vardette you join the wider track and AV2 at the cluster of farm buildings that make up Creton (1852m). Follow the paved curves of the old royal route to join the road heading W, soon with the lovely sight of Rosa dei Banchi and its snowfield (SW). An easy 40min climbing gradually will see you at the parking area and cluster of signposts where the track enters the lush flowered pasture basin of Dondena, well above the tree line now.

Proceed past summer huts and old barracks to the concrete building of Rif. Dondena (2200m). *Though it bears no resemblance to the royal hunting lodge from which it was converted, the lack of atmosphere*

*is amply compensated for by the hospitality and homestyle cooking which
includes "polenta concia" (corn meal porridge layered with melted butter
and local cheese), and tasty roasts such as rabbit.*

*After-dinner strolls in the dark are best confined to the immediate
vicinity of the refuge as this used to be a favourite meeting place for witches.
In one episode a newborn baby was spirited away from its cot in the village
of Donnas near Hône-Bard, but subsequently rescued by a peasant with the
unlikely name of Napolion.*

(Allow about 1h45min in the opposite direction.)

Stage Two: to Rif. Miserin (1h30min) and Finestra di Champorcher (1h)

Follow yellow and black waymarking W along the jeep-width track
up the widening valley. (A variant, path n.7 for Lago Miserin, heads
S at first and is slightly shorter.) Well above the tree line, spreads of
flowers including edelweiss, which betray the presence of limestone,
and coloured rock (greenstone for instance) brighten the landscape.
Overhead power lines and pylons are constant if unobtrusive
companions.

(A good 40min up is the signed turn-off for Mont Glacier, N.
Time and weather permitting, the scenic 3186m peak is worth the 3h
ascent, classified "average" on difficulty. The path goes via Lago
Gelé and Col Fussi, before a brief descent, then heading NE for the
summit.)

About 1h is the junction for the direct route to Finestra di
Champorcher (straight on W) whereas left (SW) is the better used
track (doubling as access for the Electricity Commission maintenance
staff) for Lago Miserin and the refuge. Shortcuts save you several
wide curves. You climb out onto the undulating pastures of the glen
housing lovely Lago Miserin (2582m), with the gentle contour of
romantic sounding Rosa dei Banchi S, the most prominent if modest
(3164m) peak in the whereabouts. *The name Rosa, widely used in Valle
d'Aosta, means glacier (as per Monte Rosa), whereas Banchi comes from
a local word for white. The intriguing structure of the church-sanctuary
Notre Dame des Neiges, or Madonna della Neve, is unusually tall and
asymmetric, but is only usually open on August 5th for the well-attended
procession. Spacious historic Rif. Miserin (somewhat run-down and not
particularly clean nowadays) was originally constructed as a hospice for*

travellers such as mine workers crossing from Champorcher to Cogne.

Cross the front end of the lake via the dam wall and take the clear path across rubble and probably late-lying snow in gradual ascent eastish, cutting up the left-hand side of the main valley. Not far below the pass you join the direct route from Rif. Dondena (the continuation of the king's track), among masses of bright blooms such as purple saxifrage. A stone hut stands to the side of the pass, but its precarious state means it is unsuitable for anything but emergency shelter. Finestra (window) di Champorcher (2828m), also referred to as Fenêtre and Colle, opens up between Bec Costazza (SE) and Tour Ponton (N).

Beneath the pylons here are dry stone walls for resting on and admiring the wide-ranging views, as you'll probably see ibex doing on higher rocks: NW is Punta Tersiva, the clear point of the Grivola stands out due W, Gran Paradiso WSW, and the Torre del Gran Pietro SW, to mention a few.

Yeld and Coolidge went to the bother of informing their readers that the pass "was the scene of a skirmish, in September, 1799, between the French and Austrian troops", at the time of Napoleon's Second Italian Campaign.

(About 2h for this stage in the reverse direction.)

Stage Three: descent via Vallon de Bardoney (2h) to Lillaz (1h30min)

The clear path descends easily in wide curves (W then SW) this lovely ample valley, Vallon de Urtier. The thickly flowered slopes (enormous violets and the yellow flowers of creeping avens dominate) are pitted with marmot burrows. Just over 30min will see you at A. Peradza (2526m), below scattered evidence of small-scale mining activity near the foundations for a new refuge, abandoned recently as authorisation was lacking. Due S is the Cima di Peradza, its small glacier feeding cascades.

In early summer dense carpets of white ranunculus and pasque flowers accompany you down a brief stretch of wide vehicle track and over a torrent to where the path resumes - signposted turn-off left. A brief climb follows then a traverse of yet more spectacular wild flower areas, where several streams are forded (due W now).

(Some 40min down from Peradza a faded signpost points N across the stream to huts at Broillot (2340m) where it is possible to

Descending Vallon de Urtier

join the farm track for a more direct if less interesting alternative for Lillaz.)

A sharp corner left is turned, another watercourse crossed, and an unmarked junction reached - keep on the lower path. A long level stretch follows overlooking the farm road and waterfall down right. Alpenrose and juniper shrubs, not to mention numerous black vanilla orchids, precede a light wood of Arolla pine and larch (shade at last). The path eventually bears left affording glimpses up the Vallon de Bardoney, and you have to keep your eyes skinned for yellow paint splashes for the way winding down S via the Park ranger's hut then the bridge (2140m, 2h from the pass). The torrent descends in a lovely series of cascades and waterfalls.

A little further on you are joined by the path from Alpe Bardoney (see Walk 6). The torrent is now crashing down through the deep gorge on your right. Zigzags through the conifer wood lead to a clearing (intersection with a farm track). Close to the main Torrent Ayasse now, you soon reach a wooden bridge after which is the hamlet of Gollie (1830m, drinking water). With just over 30min to go, the valley narrows and immense slabs of glacially smoothed rock are passed, above the Lillaz waterfalls (see Walk 5). Black water piping accompanies the path some way, and catches up with you again down on the road at the small power plant.

The bus stop at Lillaz (1617m) coincides with the start of the road, while the main part of the village (accommodation) is on the opposite bank of the torrent.

(Reverse timing - some 4h30min.)

Path to Cogne (40min)
For Alta Via 2 walkers and those who miss the bus, head down the road from the Lillaz car park. Keep to the left of the road and onto a wide track. At the hamlet of Champlong (10min), AV2 turns left over a bridge then down through pleasant wood alongside the torrent. *The banal-looking shrine passed shortly is dated 1842 and houses the surprising painted announcement that the Bishop of Aosta conceded sinners an illegible number of days' indulgence for every "Ave Maria" they recited there.*

The path finally joins the road to enter the lace-making centre of Cogne, with plenty of shops, as well as a well-stocked Tourist Office in the main square.

(Timing for opposite direction: 45min.)

RIF. DONDENA tel:0125/37206 Private, sleeps 24 (30/6-30/9)
RIF. MISERIN C/O tel:0125/37130. Private (owned by the Champorcher Parish), sleeps 40. Always open with bedding and cooking facilities, but only manned and meals provided in August.
TOURIST OFFICE CHAMPORCHER tel:0125/37134
TOURIST OFFICE COGNE tel:0165/74040

WALK 5 *(see map C, p.52)*
Vallon di Cogne - The Lillaz Waterfalls

---

via Lillaz - lower, middle and upper waterfalls - Lillaz.
Total walking time: **1h30min**

This is an easy circular walk with only brief climbs. It could seem superfluous to devote a whole itinerary to a visit of this series of three waterfalls, but they are only revealed in their grandiosity (and 150m drop) once the path has been followed in its entirety all the way up to the highest fall. A mere glimpse is offered from Lillaz itself. No difficulty is involved, but as several stretches are devoid of guard rail protection and wind-borne spray often makes the terrain slippery, youngsters should be kept within reach. The circuit is feasible from early summer right through to autumn, however the falls are obviously at their most impressive when the snow is melting, spring and early summer.

Access: Lillaz can be reached by July to mid-September (SVAP company) buses from Cogne, or 45min on foot. By car, drive all the way up to Lillaz.

At the bus stop and car park at Lillaz (1617m) signposting for the "cascate" sends you across the bridge then through the small village. Take the first left through to a picnic area. The wide track follows the bank of the torrent virtually to the foot of the lowest fall. You climb up through waist-height shrub vegetation to several good viewing points of the drop.

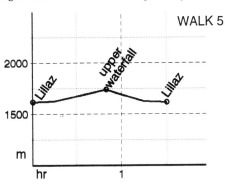

The path heads right at first and climbs the dry hillside before curving back and leading to the area of the middle fall, with some crystal clear azure pools. Not far above, via several stretches of wooden railing, is a giddy bridge over the torrent as it gushes through its picturesque rock channel.

From here the very top fall can be reached by way of a flowered meadow (martagon lilies abound), the far end of which gives access to a short clamber down to an idyllic sheltered wooded area of tranquil pools among boulders. Weary feet are instantly revived when bathed in the invigorating water. The highest fall is in the background, thundering out from a rock cleft.

To complete the circuit, instead of returning the same way, go back to the lower edge of the meadow and turn right. A yellow-marked path (n.14) leads between enormous glacially-modelled rocks and light wood to emerge in vegetable gardens on a hillside shrouded in rosebay-willow-herb. You soon join the main descent path from Vallon de Urtier. It comes out near the torrent once more, and shortly down the dirt road is the Lillaz bus stop and car park you started from.

TOURIST OFFICE COGNE tel:0165/74040

WALK 6 *(see map C, p.52)*
Vallon di Cogne - Lago di Loie

via Lillaz - Lago di Loie (2h15min) - Alpe di Bardoney (1h) - Gollie (1h15min) - Lillaz (30min)
Total walking time: **5h (1 day suggested)**

This beautiful round trip is suitable for all the family and is a good walk to start off a holiday. The only "difficulty" is the steepish climb in the first part. As well as a variety of landscapes, there are plenty of panoramic points and views range as far as Mont Blanc. The lake area, brightly flowered, is popular for picnics, though those interested in observing the chamois that frequent the surrounding mountainsides and crests are advised to arrive early. Early summer

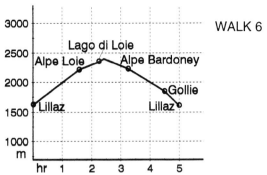

WALK 6

to late autumn is feasible. During the return descent a detour can be made to take in the magnificent Lillaz waterfalls.
Access: see Walk 5.

Stage One: via Alpe Loie (1h35min) to Lago di Loie (40min)
From the bus stop and car park at Lillaz (1617m) cross the bridge (signposting for n.12) right into the village (small hotels, food shops and fountains). Follow the signs for the "Cascate" first left past Albergo Cascate to the torrent. Soon after a picnic area where the waterfall path continues alongside the torrent, n.12 starts its climb up right heading S. This is one of the few woods in the area and the Arolla pines, larch and fir provide welcome shade while alpenrose, bilberries and a variety of wild flowers brighten the undergrowth. After some 1h30min of steady and in parts steepish climbing up the right side of a trickling waterfall, you emerge onto what was previously pasture, near the ruins of the Alpe Loie (2216m). Detour briefly to the right (watch out for marmots) to the point overlooking Valeille. Past Cogne in the distant NW-WNW is M. Blanc, the Grivola point closer WNW, while opposite SW is Punta Fenilia, not to mention the collection of snowed and iced peaks S up Vallon di Valeille.

Above the tree line now, the marked path heads E across rubble for the final uphill stretch across easy open grass and rock terrain. Check the rocks up right occasionally as solo male chamois rest there, at a distance from the herds of females with their young around the lake.

Blue-green Lago di Loie (2354m) itself nestles in a cup-shaped basin overlooked by grey points such as Punta di Loie SSW. The green sloping banks are covered by purple asters and black vanilla orchids, whereas the northern bank consists of glacially smoothed rocks. The area lends itself to picnics and a (quick) swim is definitely feasible. *The name, also spelt Loye, comes from "Lex" locally used to refer to the large slabs of rock used for roofing.*

(For this stage in the opposite direction, 1h30min should suffice.)

Stage Two: traverse to Alpe Bardoney (1h) and descent to Gollie (1h15min) hence Lillaz (30min)

Path n.12 follows the left side of the lake then climbs to another superb viewpoint (10min) from where Punta Tersiva is ENE. As the path bears E, mostly on level ground, the peaks above delightful Vallon de Bardoney come into view, namely Punta Nera E, then Torre Lavina with its remnant glacier SE. You descend towards a sea of green and gold vegetation in a shallow marsh. The path circles the wetter parts - beware of squelchy shortcuts through the cotton grass. Over a rise the path veers left to join the main valley route near the cascading torrent. From here it's 10min up right past "roches moutonnées" to the stone buildings of active summer farm Alpe Bardoney (2232m, dairy products on sale). The valley widens considerably here providing lush green pasture. *When the livestock are not around, marmots are more evident. The name Bardoney means a concentration of Rumex Acetosella, otherwise known as sheep's sorrel.*

For the descent, return to the junction and continue down (NE) the valley on the wide path. The torrent on the right rushes through deep passages before a lovely long drop into a blue pool. Some 30min down you join the Alta Via 2 path (from Finestra di Champorcher) and waymarking is a yellow-black triangle. It's NW now down through a mixed conifer wood alive with song birds. After intersecting a farm access dirt track just above Torrente Urtier, a wide bridge crosses the watercourse and reaches a hamlet (drinking water). Keep left on the path (whereas the wide track goes up to meet the restricted traffic road from Lillaz) and around to a signed path junction below the hamlet of Gollie (1854m). With ups and downs through tall vegetation, several detours are necessary to avoid crumbled stretches of the original path, and you emerge into the lower valley with a series of hidden waterfalls on your left. To see the justifiably well-known Lillaz Cascate at close quarters, you can slot into the waterfall circuit as an alternative return. After the stretch of black water pipe there is an intersection of dirt paths (one comes in from the asphalt road to your right), and the left branch leads through vegetable gardens to the upper fall (see Walk 5). Should you miss this turn-off, a few minutes down path n.14 also leads around left to join the circuit.

For the straightforward descent to Lillaz, keep on the path that winds down through scrubby wood to the valley floor near the torrent. A short stretch right along the road past a small hydro-electric power station brings you out at the Lillaz car park and bus stop.

(In the reverse direction, allow 3h for this stage.)

TOURIST OFFICE COGNE tel:0165/74040

WALK 7 *(see map C, p.52)*
Vallon di Valeille - Capanna Arolla

---

via Lillaz - Vallon di Valeille - Capanna Arolla (2h15min) - Lillaz (1h30min)
Total walking time: **3h45min (1 day suggested)**

A straightforward family day walk in tranquil Vallon di Valeille, a rather desolate valley, nowhere near as popular with visitors (or as spectacular) as Valnontey for example. The destination, Capanna Arolla, once a shepherd's hut but now National Park property, is set on a panoramic platform in an excellent spot for wildlife, ibex in particular. The name comes from the Arolla pine, presumably found in the valley in greater numbers in previous times.

Experienced walkers can extend this route by continuing up the unfrequented (and not always well-marked) path with several uncertain stretches, to the high pass, Colle Arolla (2892m). Its strategic importance in hunting days explains the old hunting posts and the traces of a wider game track, still evident. From the pass it

63

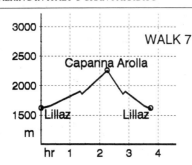

is possible to descend eastwards into Val Bardoney, and after a stretch N to Alpe Bardoney, is the link into Walk 6 to return to Lillaz - allow a good 7h in all.

Access: see Walk 5.

Stage One: via Vallone di Valeille to Capanna Arolla (2h15min)
Both the bus terminal and car park are on the northernmost bank of the wide Torrente Grand Eyvia at Lillaz (1617m). Once across the main bridge (S) and through the small settlement (including a food shop) you'll see old orange signposting for Capanna Arolla (n.15a) indicating a dirt lane left, before the camping ground. Past a beautiful cascade the track curves left then back towards the torrent, crossing it after 20min total.

Gentle silent round-sided Vallone di Valeille is revealed now, its U-shape a legacy of its ancient glacial past. (*Its scree-lined flanks were further gouged out by terrible rivers of earth and rock, dislodged by the torrential rain in the autumn of 1993. The valley floor, once good pasture, is now essentially pebbles with the occasional gigantic boulder.*) The valley is sealed at its far southern end by a light grey high rock wall with the prominent point of Punta d'Ondezana SSW. The underlying platform hosts Ghiacciaio di Valeille. A little closer SSE, beneath imposing Punta delle Sengie, is the glacier of the same name (*probably from the Latin "cingulum" for grassy belt set above or in the middle of a chasm*).

Wide path n.15, originally one of the king's game tracks, proceeds on the right-hand side of the torrent. Marmots, the occasional larch and plenty of raspberries for late summer visitors, characterise the easy, gentle ascent across several lateral gullies. As you climb, there are views back N to the Colonna mine buildings above Cogne, lofty and distant as a Tibetan monastery.

Some 1h from the bridge is a signed path junction (at about 1900m) where you head down left on n.15a towards the torrent. At the time of writing a temporary plank bridge was in place, but work

Temporary bridge crossing in Valeille - Walk 7
Stone pillar marker en route to Punta Fenilia - Walk 9

Lago di Lauson reflecting Torre del Gran San Pietro and Roccia Viva - Walk 11

Roman bridge at Pondel - Walk 15

was under way on a higher and sturdier construction, much needed.

Capanna Arolla is visible now on a spur due E (some 50min away). Past the previous site of A. Valeille (2258m), now all but disappeared, a clear path, marked by high cairns at first, starts its stiff zigzagging through green alder bushes and other shrub vegetation. A series of stone steps takes you leftish to a grassy shoulder overlooking a cascade, then right beneath dark rock outcrops. Marmots abound, then as you climb up around the corner, young inquisitive ibex will probably be keeping a check on your progress from the rocks above. The marvellous grass platform is soon reached where Capanna Arolla (2258m) occupies a commanding position, including a view SSW towards Torre del Gran San Pietro. *The hut is usually manned in summer by a Park ranger, in the heart of an area favoured by ptarmigan as well as sizeable herds of ibex.*

Stage Two: descent to Lillaz (1h30min)
As per the ascent.

From the lower Valeille bridge where the vehicle track starts, instead of crossing the torrent right, keep straight ahead on path n.14. It soon drops close to a dramatic cascade and via a wooden bridge emerges alongside the camping ground, just before the turn-off for the ascent.

TOURIST OFFICE COGNE tel:0165/74040

WALK 8 *(see map D, p.66)*
Vallon de Grauson -
Lakes, Edelweiss and the Old Mines

---

via Gimillan - Vallon de Grauson - Biv. Grauson (2h30min) - Laghi di Lussert (2h30min return time) - Passo d'Invergneux (2h15min) - old Colonna mines (2h30min) - Cogne (1h15min)
Total walking time: **11h (2 days suggested)**

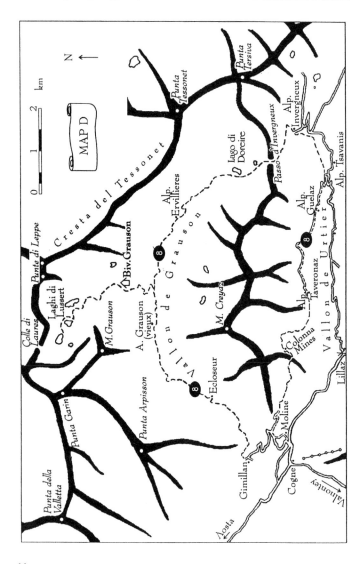

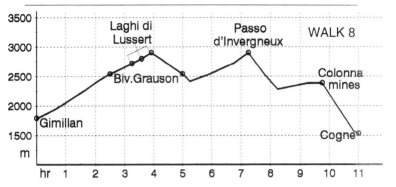

While not included in the National Park area, lovely Vallon de Grauson and its high altitude lakes are well worth a visit. The pastures in the lower reaches are still used, but luckily for walkers no road has been put in, unlike Vallon de Urtier. Wild animals are not as easily observable as in the Park domain, but once you're out of the range of the grazing cows and their accompanying dogs, both marmots and shy chamois are likely, in addition to the silent gliding raptors or even the lammergeier vulture which local reports give as an occasional visitor. Charr, a type of alpine trout, survive in the chilly waters of the lakes. Yet another reason to visit the valley is the incredible variety of wild flowers, and unusual concentrations of (protected) edelweiss.

As well as a rewarding day return outing as far as the lower lake, a perfect family trip could include an overnight stay at comfortable bivouac hut Bivacco Grauson. It is sometimes referred to on maps as Biv. Tentori in memory of Carlo Tentori, a frequent visitor to the area and whose family had it restored. It consists of the upper floor of a run-down shepherds' hut recently converted into delightful and roomy quarters with beds and blankets, a gas stove, fully equipped kitchen, WC and running water, and is usually kept locked. Intending lodgers need only drop in at the sports shop, Ezio Sport in the centre of Cogne, to book and collect the key. There is no charge for accommodation, but donations towards maintenance costs can be left in the "offerte" box in the hut itself.

Paths and waymarking are clear and straightforward as far as the lakes. Only in the beautiful solitary upper reaches of Vallon de

Grauson en route to Passo d'Invergneux does orientation become a little problematic as path markers are few and far between.

The descent route goes via Vallon de Urtier and Cogne's abandoned mines, preceded unfortunately by a monotonous stretch of farm road. Should the mines not interest you, a more direct route to Lillaz is also possible, cutting nearly 2h off total walking time.

A visit to the Colonna mines, said to be among the highest in Europe, also makes an interesting day trip from Cogne. A round trip is possible by following path n.24 in ascent (allow 2h) signposted from the Cogne-Lillaz road below Moline, then taking the descent path described in Stage Five.

Access: The quiet village of Gimillan, also spelt Gimmilian, with several small hotels, is a winding scenic 5min (3.5km) bus trip N from Cogne. The (SVAP company) service runs July - mid-September. The alternative exit point Lillaz is similarly served by bus in summer. Car owners can park in either Gimillan or Cogne.

Stage One: via Vallon de Grauson to Biv. Grauson (2h30min)
From the car park and bus stop at Gimillan (1787m) take the first road uphill right after Hotel Tersiva to a batch of yellow signposts. In common with several others at the start, the path n.8/9a threads its way NE between emerald green meadows and alongside gushing irrigation channels. After several changes of direction, the path, paved in parts, joins a variant from the village. Past a whitewashed shrine (20min) and an unmarked turn-off left, the path moves closer to the watercourse and gradually enters Vallon de Grauson, the vegetation reverting to its natural state.

A bridge over the watercourse (Torrente Grauson) leads past farm houses (Ecloseur, 1947m) and into the lightly wooded pastoral zone. Further on a flight of steps cut into the rock flank climbs to the right of a waterfall (some 1h15min this far), a good spot to pause and admire the view back SW over Cogne to the glaciers at the head of Valnontey. In an easterly direction now you proceed through a series of flowered pasture terraces dotted with shepherds' huts and the last stands of larch. After a metal cross on a rise is a level stretch to a sizeable grouping of stone huts known as Alp. de Grauson (vieux), 2271m. The path soon crosses to the left-hand side of the torrent and your passage will undoubtedly raise brilliant clouds of tiny metallic blue butterflies from their puddles.

As the valley widens Punta Tersiva and its modest glacier come into view ESE, and about the same time you reach a signposted junction - turn up left (N) for Laghi di Lussert (Biv. Grauson is not actually signposted) and the final 25min climb through pasture to the bivouac hut. The entrance to Biv. Grauson is "hidden" at the rear of three low-standing corrugated iron-roofed huts at 2540m. Graceful, pointed Grivola is in the distance WSW.

(A good 1h45min in descent.)

Stage Two: Laghi di Lussert - lago inferiore (45min), lago intermedio (20min), lago superiore (20min) - 2h30min total return time

Take the path signposted for Laghi di Lussert along the front of the buildings for the climb N over a series of hillocks and rises and into the ample green expanse of this peaceful side valley. (A variant path keeps left following the torrent and the two join up before the first lake.) There are vast flattened and glacially smoothed expanses of rock to be crossed, and an incongruous oversized wall of rubble is invading the opposite side. Though out of sight, a small glacier, Ghiacciaio di Lussert, is the force bulldozing what is actually frontal moraine. Other signs of glacial action are the scooped-out armchair-shaped cirques that house the lakes.

When you reach an unmarked junction further ahead, keep straight on for the lowest and largest lake (lago inferiore) - 5min away, beyond the crest at 2721m (45min this far).

Back at the junction, take the northern fork for the second lake. The path, narrower and steeper now, climbs quickly up crumbly loose terrain then follows a ridge. Twenty minutes later it emerges at a squarish boulder on the broad shores of the inky middle lake (lago intermedio, 2800m). Fed by a stream trickling from the upper lake, it occupies a steep-backed cirque amidst pink-red rock, blackened on the surface. Yet another delightful flowered picnic spot.

For the final stretch to the top lake, follow the yellow arrows right along the shore to where clear marking guides you up the rocky walled sides and NW into the next desolate cirque. *Snow persists well into summer at this altitude along with resolute gentians, daisies, over-sized yellow-centred violets and tiny spiders around the shore of this highest lake* (lago superiore, 2907m). *Only the splash of the occasional fish surfacing breaks the silence.* WSW is the pronounced peak of Punta Garin.

The slight depression visible NW, Colle di Laures (3036m), can be reached by following the faint traces of path and venturing across fallen rock. Views N and more icy lakes are the reward. Allow 20min extra time.

The return to Biv. Grauson via the three lakes is the same route as the ascent.

Stage Three: ascent to Passo d'Invergneux (2h15min)

From the hut, 15min will see you back down at the path junction in Vallon de Grauson. Turn left as n.8 crosses a stream then climbs gradually E across lush green slopes into the peaceful ample upper valley. In the vicinity of a nearby cluster of basic huts (2418m) still used by shepherds, edelweiss are prolific together with purple asters and strongly scented black vanilla orchids. You soon drop down right nearer to the main torrent, but keep to its left-hand side for some time. The path as such disappears regularly, and you're left with a very faint series of markings on the rare stones - occcasional yellow arrows and stripes, in addition to yellow/black Alta Via 4 triangles.

Some 35min from the first junction should see you at the abandoned huts of Alp. Ervillieres (2519m), where the pasture has been taken over by marmots and stinging nettles. Head right here but instead of the tempting torrent crossing, keep on the left bank and climb up to the ridge. Pointed stones have been set upright to guide walkers across the open expanses and shortly lead through an evocative strange oval of stones. With several side stream crossings, the route maintains a SE direction, up and down numerous hillocks to where another wider watercourse is reached. After this the terrain becomes rockier and covered with vast masses of debris known as drumlins and kames, glacially transported material. The path, clearer now, climbs due S to the westernmost end of Lago di Doreire (2731m).

For the final 30min in ascent, you resume the SE tendency and climb towards the pass through a distinctly different vegetation band - flowers for the most part, tiny brightly coloured varieties. *The alpine moon-daisies and ranunculus form fresh patches of white, tiny gentians contribute their unique intense royal blue and forget-me-nots an exquisite sky-blue.* From a small lake on the left of the path, often dried up by midsummer, is an interesting view of the lower lake with an extensive dark NW-running ridge, Cresta del Tessonet, in the background. Helpful cairns lead you the final easy metres to wide flat Passo d'Invergneux (2905m, also known as Col des Hévergnes) with its marvellous outlook. *The name means "wintering", a reference to the valley's first residents, shepherds from the Valle Soana (SE), who stayed over instead of returning home after the annual transhumance.* Mountain-wise now, Punta Tersiva is ENE, Punta Garin NW, Torre Lavin S, and you have a long clear view S down Vallon di Bardoney, not to mention ample Vallon de Urtier with its winding tracks and watercourses. And the chances are that you'll have it all to yourself. (1h30min in descent.)

Stage Four: descent to Vallon de Urtier (1h) and the old Colonna mines (1h30min)
A narrow but clear path (7a) drops down left (SE) across the

Colonna mines and view up Valeille

flowered rubble slope which soon gives way to earth and grass once more. Unfortunately at the time of writing there was no trace of path n.7 that the maps show heading SW, so keep on this path for some 20min in gradual descent as far as a grassy basin beneath Punta Tersiva. (Adventurous walkers can cut down the slopes in the direction of Alp Guelaz at 2336m to join the boring road described below.) Then turn off and make your way down S to the Alpage marked on maps as Invergneux/Hévergnes (15min). From here a faint path cuts the wide curves of the vehicle track towards the bridge below. Without actually going as far as the bridge, keep right (W) and look for the marked path (7a) alongside the torrent leading down to another bridge and dirt road (erroneously shown on the opposite bank of the torrent on the maps). Here at 2280m is a signed path junction (2280m, 1h this far from the pass, compared to some 2h in the opposite direction).

(*Alternative exit to Lillaz (1h15min):* this farm access road leads all the way down W to Lillaz (1617m), and while a little monotonous, it is feasible as an alternative descent at this point. Allow around 1h15min for the 6km.)

To continue on to the mines, take the turn-off (n.7) right a couple of minutes down the road. A tedious 1h of wide gravel in company of overhead power lines and enormous pylons follows. Essentially W, you pass several farms and cross two watercourses. Once Alp. de Taveronaz (2388m) is reached, the next 30min are quite different. A path takes over among thick clumps of edelweiss, the side valleys suddenly open up S as far as the Gran Paradiso group, and soon around a corner you see the huddle of constructions which, from a distance, could almost be mistaken for a Tibetan monastery. Raptors and cawing alpine choughs wheel around.

The ex-mine area called Colonna (2387m) has now fallen into disuse and is fenced off, but fresh yellow arrows lead you over and around the main buildings. The open-air mine itself, developed on this southern flank of Monte Creyaz, whose pure magnetite mass yielded an iron concentration of some 55%, can be reached by following the path that climbs the steep mountainside ENE up to an altitude of 2500m.

The upper reaches of the valley are pitifully bare in terms of vegetation, as trees fed the countless small-scale furnaces set up to smelt the iron ore before the mine was taken over by a large company and the steel works established in Aosta. Operations ceased in 1979.

(Similar timing for the reverse direction, ie. 1h30min.)

Stage Five: descent via Moline to Cogne (1h15min)

The path, exposed briefly, drops steeply hugging the white cliff face to a path junction (10min). Ignore n.7 off right and keep left down (unmarked path) through the springy dwarf mountain pines. You descend quickly in tight zigzags then cut W across the mountainside (reinforced sections of path) and soon reach another set of mine buildings. Here blue arrows send you between buildings via a series of precarious ladders. You keep on relentlessly downwards past other buildings and pylons, and where a near-vertical trolley line terminates in a spacious shed, enter via the ladder and out the other side onto a wide white vehicle track (50min from Colonna). Heading decisively NW, this soon joins up with the road from Gimillan. But you can soon leave it by turning left down to the Moline "Museo mineralogico" with exhibits and photos to testify to the miners' way of living. Moline (1576m), which starts here and spreads downhill, was a model mining village, and the name means "mill". *Historical records date back as far as 15th century. Raw material was transported this far by sled in early times before the construction of the mechanised cableway. As of the 1920s it was forwarded to Aosta's iron foundry by narrow gauge electric train. The line burrowed beneath the Punta del Drinc via a 7km tunnel, to terminate near Pila (Plan Praz, the intermediate cable car station) above Aosta, where another cableway took over. Re-adaptation of the rail line for passenger services with an estimated capacity of 400 pax/hr is under way, though contested by supporters of a project for a cable car from Epinel via the Couiss crest to connect with the upper Pila station. Promotors of both projects are spurred on by the frequent closure of Cogne's narrow access road by landslides or avalanches.*

The secondary road leads to the valley floor where you turn right for the centre of Cogne (1534m).

(Allow some 2h30min in the opposite direction climbing from Cogne to Colonna, involving some 850m in ascent.)

BIV. GRAUSON Private, sleeps 12. Blankets, gas stove and running water. For booking and keys, contact Ezio Sport, Cogne tel:0165/74204

TOURIST OFFICE COGNE: tel:0165/74040

WALK 9 *(see map E, p.75)*
Vallon di Cogne - Punta Fenilia

---

via **Cogne** - upper cable car station (10min) - Punta Fenilia (3h30min) - descent (2h40min) - cable car to Cogne (10min)
Total walking time: **6h10min + 20min cable car (1 day suggested)**

This excursion is a great challenge, if rather long for a single day. It culminates in a shortish but tiring climb of considerable difficulty for an average walker. The reward, however, is a marvellously panoramic peak that you'll only have to share with the resident ibex. At 3053m, Punta Fenilia affords sweeping views of a semicircle of glacier-scape SE-S-NW taking in a series of important peaks.

The ascent is described here starting with the cable car from Cogne (1534m) which saves some 600m in ascent. The operating times (9am-5.45pm, late June to mid-September) just allow sufficient time to complete the route. Remember that walking times mean in good conditions, and include neither rest stops nor wrong turns. In early summer with snow it will take a little longer.

Note: a shorter easy circuit is also possible, though of course a little less panoramic. From the cable car arrival station follow signposting right in ascent through the wood for the nearby Belvedere, hence path n.17 to Montzeuc (2333m). This name, from "goat without horns", is due to its rounded shape which contrasts with the other pointed peaks around. Proceed E to the junction with the main itinerary (near the top of a ski lift), from where you return W and down through the wood back to the cable car. 2h should cover the complete circuit.

Access: Cogne is served by year-round buses from Aosta (SVAP company). Drivers can park at the cable car station - follow signs for the "Telecabina".

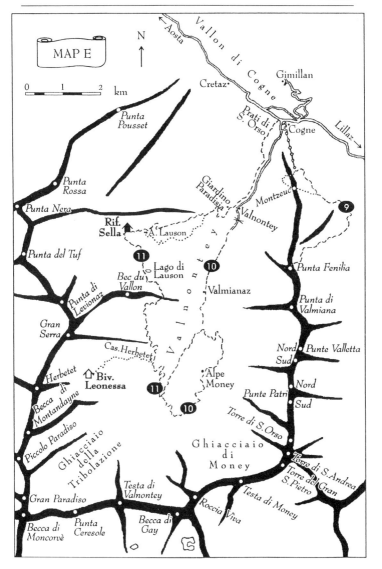

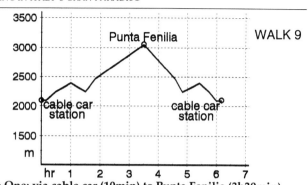

Stage One: via cable car (10min) to Punta Fenilia (3h30min)
The modern bubble cabins glide S up through conifer wood and
there are interesting views over the valley of the layout of Cogne's
various mine sites, now abandoned.

From the bar above the arrival station (2100m) take the path
(n.17) around left to a wide track on a level (the right branch climbs
to the Belvedere). Yellow arrows direct you SE through conifer
wood frequented by chamois, and along ski service trails (soon
joined by an alternative track from Cogne) and pistes to the top of
a ski lift and path junction (30min this far). Where a branch of n.17
descends from the shorter Montzeuc circuit, keep left and across the
front of this valley heaped with enormous fallen rocks and dominated
by immense tilted grey rock strata. Keep your eyes skinned for
yellow arrows or faded red marks across rocks to a steep path which
leaves the last of the larch. You climb to an iron marker pole for good
views of the valley floors including Lillaz and its series of cascades,
M. Emilius N, Punta Tersiva ENE, various glaciers and peaks SSE
down Valeille, and even M. Blanc in the distant NW. Don't be
tempted to climb to the large cairn above right, but keep straight on
to drop down diagonally left over a series of terraces, necessary in
order to get around the successive rubble-choked valley. A path
from Lillaz joins up, following which is a 30min tiring crossing over
irregular boulders brightened by clumps of red alpenrose. Once the
grassy path reappears it's not far up to an enormous stone pillar-
cum-cairn at 2472m and more views.

From here the path heads SW and it's easy-going over grassy
and brightly flowered slopes. *This zone is the haunt of herds of female*

ibex with their young, and though they may move away on your arrival, will often stay in view and perch immobile on high ridges to observe visitors at length.

After about 1h uphill you reach the rubble valley at the foot of the sweeping curve of crest including Punta Fenilia (identifiable by a whitish pole). Snow lies here well into summer. A yellow painted message on a rock informs "Fenilia salire dal colle sinistra", "climb the Fenilia peak from the col to its left", referring to the very last stretch. That is, follow the route up the middle of the basin across rock then easy rubble with a faint path visible every now and again. After about 40min as it becomes quite steep and difficult and rocks looser, make your way up to the col just left of the summit, before climbing to the marker pole itself. Extra care and a sure foot are necessary. As well as plunging views down west into Valnontey, you can enjoy the marvellous sight of the Grivola WNW, around to Gran Paradiso SW, Torre del Gran San Pietro S, Punta delle Sengie SSE, encompassing many intermediate peaks and ice fields. 3053m Punta Fenilia demands you take a breather.

Stage Two: descent (2h40min) then via cable car to Cogne (10min)
As per the ascent route.

TOURIST OFFICE COGNE tel:0165/74040

WALK 10 *(see map E, p.75)*
Valnontey - The Glacier Terrace

---

via Valnontey - Alpe Money (3h) - upper Valnontey (1h15min) - Valnontey (1h35min)
Total walking time: **5h50min (1 day suggested)**

This is a superb and popular day outing during which every ounce of effort spent in climbing the 650 steep metres to the Alpe Money is fully repaid by the ample magnificence of the cascading Tribolazione glacier beneath the impressive chain of peaks from the Herbetet around to include Gran Paradiso and Roccia Viva. Closer at hand it's not unusual to see ibex grazing on the high slopes even

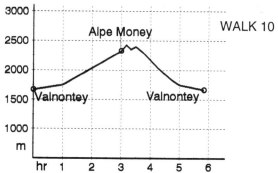

in midsummer.

While the initial part of the walk along the floor of Valnontey follows a wide easy track, the ascent to Alpe Money is steep and tiring in places and unsuitable for youngsters. Adverse weather would make it more difficult and of course spoil the views.

Note: if you set out with the intention of walking the complete circuit, it is advisable to check beforehand on the condition, or existence, of the bridge in upper Valnontey preceding the 2040m path junction in Stage Two. The descent involves several minor torrent crossings where, if the worst comes to the worst, it's a matter of getting your feet wet. The main torrent, however, is a serious affair. The flow can be strong and impetuous with a high level on early summer afternoons. Crossing slippery logs in the absence of a bridge is not everyone's cup of tea. Apart from the disastrous flooding and consequent landslides in late September 1993, it is not unusual for bridges, often simply planks, to be washed away in spring, and local workers are often kept busy with such maintenance at the start of the tourist season.

Note: Valnontey is both the name of the settlement where the walk starts in addition to being the name of the valley.

Access: summer buses (SVAP company, July to mid-September) from Cogne to Valnontey, or 45min on foot (see Walk 12). Drivers can leave their cars in the central parking area.

Stage One: ascent to Alpe Money (3h)
The bus terminates at the parking area at Valnontey (1666m, several

hotels and camping grounds, shop). The promising view S of the glaciers is a hint of what's to come. A few minutes upstream at the bridge is signposting for Alp Money. Take the road along the left-hand side of the torrent to a camping ground - no private traffic beyond this point. It's a pleasant stroll past several clusters of huts including Valmianaz (1729m), and through conifer wood on the banks of the wide white torrent. A total of 1h will see you at the turn-off (left) for path n.20.

The climb, stiff at times, is a constant series of tight zigzags. Beneath the meagre larch trees are pink alpenrose, wine red martagon lilies and fresh yellow gentians. At the tree limit there's a swing around left to the first of several moderately exposed passages, then after further climbing, the path resumes its (right) southwards bearing swinging around to coast across dry mountainsides. The panorama verges on breathtaking but broadens even more as you proceed. There are several rushing streams to be crossed via wobbly stones followed by ups and downs, then the junction for "Biv. Money" (another good 1h30min to the yellow bivouac hut set at 2872m and visible from the Alpe - access restricted to energetic walkers with some climbing experience). Ignore the turn-off and keep on to the actual pasture area of Alpe Money (2325m). Preceding the few abandoned shepherds' huts still standing are vast grey-brown slabs, lime green with lichen, of glacially smoothed rock - a reminder that the glaciers ahead once submerged the entire valley and ice masses slid along these flanks so high up from the present valley floor.

The place name Money, commonly found in Valle d'Aosta for shared pastures, is believed to be pre-Roman. Equivalents evidently exist in the Irish "moin" and Gaelic "moneth". As far as legendary times went, a ghostly horseman attired in green was known to appear at Col Money (SSE) and descend in great leaps over the glacier to play havoc with the milking cows, as revenge for the bad treatment of a young shepherd.

Due west over Valnontey are the Casolari dell'Herbetet, below the triangular peak of the same name, then in the (near 180°) sea of ice the rock protagonists are Gran Paradiso SW, Testa di Valnontey SSW, Roccia Viva S, to name a few of these monumental mountains.

(Just over 2h are required for this stage in the opposite direction.)

Alpe Money and the glacier-bound head of Valnontey

Stage Two: descent to upper Valnontey (1h15min) hence Valnontey (1h35min)

The odd yellow arrow points S from the huts toward a brief climb. After coasting across mixed rock and grass terrain beneath the glacier (Ghiacciaio di Money), the path, not always clear, descends in a SW direction towards the upper reaches of Valnontey. A good halfway is a steep descent down a sort of earth-rubble ridge, and you keep diagonally left. Several icy streams need to be crossed before the main torrent where there will hopefully be a replacement for the suspended bridge that was wrenched from its moorings several years back. On the other side a clear path leads N through the scrubby green alder to the junction at 2040m where you keep right (n.23 descends from Casolari dell'Herbetet, Walk 11). Easier and wider now in winding descent, the path follows the left bank of the torrent to a sturdy wooden bridge Pont de l'Erfaulet (1830m, 30min), then soon reaches the n.20 junction for Alpe Money. From here continue straight down the main path as per the ascent in Stage One (50min to Valnontey).

(Allow at least 3h30min in ascent for this stage.)

TOURIST OFFICE COGNE tel:0165/74040

> **WALK 11** *(see map E, p.75)*
> ## *Valnontey - A Spectacular Traverse*

**via Valnontey - Rif. Sella (2h30min) - Casolari dell'Herbetet
(2h30min) - Valnontey (2h20min)**
Total walking time: **7h20min + 2h15min for optional side trip
(2 days suggested)**

The route from Rif. Sella to the Casolari dell'Herbetet huts is one of
the most spectacular itineraries in the Park. The path coasts at a
dizzy 2500m along the western flank of Valnontey, while
breathtaking panoramas onto the immense glaciers and icefalls
southwards improve with every step. In addition the zone is
densely populated with wildlife - incredibly approachable ibex,
chamois and marmots. While the traverse itself is not suitable for
beginners due to several exposed lengths (and inadvisable for
anyone in low cloud or bad weather), the first stage is a wonderful
family day trip in itself, also possible in combination with a variant
descent (total 4h10min). Summer (July to late September) means
seeing the area at its best without snow, though the first stage as far
as the refuge is feasible at other times, conditions permitting.

An overnight stay at Rif. Sella is strongly recommended as it
gives more time for wildlife observation late afternoon or early
morning in the vicinity of the refuge and the nearby lake. Luckily
the hut operates as early as from Easter for ski tourers, right through
to the close of September.

An optional side trip is given from Casolari dell'Herbetet to Biv.
Leonessa at 2910m. The bivouac hut is always open, but intending
users must be fully equipped with sleeping and cooking gear and
food. Water is usually available in the vicinity.

Another point of interest: the Giardino Botanico Alpino
"Paradisia", the Alpine Botanical Garden established in 1955 and
named after St. Bruno's lily "Paradisia liliastrum", is a mere 5min
stroll from Valnontey. Boasting over 1500 labelled alpine plant
species in a 10,000 sq.m area, it is open to the public from early June
to mid-September (9.30-12.30am, 2.30-6.30pm).

Access: see Walk 10.

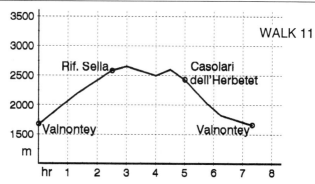

Stage One: ascent to Rif. Sella (2h30min)

Just up from the main car park and bus stop at Valnontey, turn right across the bridge for Rif. Sella. The asphalt soon ends and a wide path (n.18) leads past the botanical garden and close to a waterfall with a wonderfully long drop. The wide, well-graded mule track is still used by the pack horse that regularly plods this route loaded with supplies for the refuge. Wide zigzags lead steadily up the dry hot mountainside, meagre shade offered by the larches. About 50min up is a wooden bridge to the left at approx. 2000m - the variant descent returns here. Further up out of the wood is a bench and signpost at 2200m (a good 30min from the bridge) where the valley widens considerably.

Ibex, not to mention noisy colonies of marmots devouring thistles and daisies, are common frequenters of this area, while chamois keep their timid distance on the other (southernmost) side of the watercourse.

The easy climb continues in wide curves past a turn-off left to Alpe Lauson farm, where dairy products are on sale, and into the middle section of the valley. On the edge is the old picturesque royal hunting lodge, reputedly the scene of full-scale partying in the hunting king's days. A little further on are the actual refuge buildings, simple yet tasteful and which blend in well with the surroundings. Rif. Vittorio Sella (2584m) was named after the highly acclaimed pioneer mountain and glacier photographer, whose black and white masterpieces from the late 1800s remain unsurpassed.

Despite its great capacity for accommodation, the refuge has a homely feel and walkers are both made welcome and fed well. Leftovers are

Old royal hunting lodge near Rif. Sella

reportedly appreciated by scavenging foxes under the cover of dark. After dinner on long light summer evenings a brief trek to the lake (see Stage Two) is in order to observe the ibex and chamois watering and feeding, not to mention the extraordinary sight of young male ibex silhouetted on prominent rock outcrops, clashing horns in mock battle. In late summer, when higher pastures have been exhausted, great herds graze tranquilly on the grass flats in the vicinity of the refuge itself.

(Allow 1h40min for this stage in descent.)

Variant descent to Valnontey via Alpe Lauson (1h40min)
For a different return on a day trip, go back a short way along the path you arrived on, to where an alternative branches right (S) off the main route via Alpe Lauson. It proceeds NE down the other side of the torrent virtually parallel to the main route, before detouring left back over the torrent to rejoin the mule track at the wooden bridge (approx. 2000m) referred to in Stage One. As the slopes are frequented by sizeable herds of chamois with their young, it goes without saying that walkers must keep to the path at all times and do nothing to disturb the wildlife, as per the National Park regulations.

Stage Two: traverse via Lago di Lauson (30min) to Casolari dell'Herbetet (2h)

From Rif. Sella head SE across the torrent and along the royal game track, wide and paved with stone (n.23), winding in gradual ascent across damp grassy terrain and glacially smoothed rock slabs. The picturesque tarn, Lago di Lauson (2656m), lies some 30min from the refuge, and its waters reflect grandiose peaks and glaciers including the prominent Torre del Gran San Pietro (SE) and around to Roccia Viva (SSE).

After an easy coast around to the next point, the hunting track comes to an abrupt end and a good but narrow path begins in brief descent (about 20min from the lake). There is a reassuring if short length of chain at the very start, but the following 30min mean ups and downs with longish, moderately exposed stretches, requiring a little extra attention. Once around the midriff of Bec du Vallon, the path widens to enter (SW) the valley dominated by Gran Serra and Punta di Levionaz. After the torrent crossing below the reduced Gran Val glacier, the path continues (S) essentially over rubble, guided by cairns. It climbs to an ample platform (at about 2600m, 2h total), a magnificent viewing point for the head of the Valnontey. The icy masses of the majestic Ghiacciaio della Tribolazione seem only a stone's throw away (SSW). The crest above it is punctuated by the Gran Paradiso peak (SW), the knob of Punta Ceresole (SSW), Testa di Valnontey and Gran Crou (S) and Becca di Gay (barely to their E).

The path now drops down the escarpment, a very brief narrow passage, to the similarly panoramic Casolari dell'Herbetet huts (2435m), which are Park property. The Herbetet peak is actually WSW from here. *Its name, also used for the side valley and other features, means small pasture area.*

(Timing for the opposite direction is 2h30min as well.)

Side-trip to Biv. Leonessa (2h15min return time)

Even better views are available from the Biv. Leonessa, the dark square hut visible high up WSW.

Uphill of the huts, n.23a is a clear mule track, part of the old royal network, zigzagging W up the right side of Vallone Herbetet. After about 1h as the terrain levels out, a path bears left (SW) across the stream and via moraine for the final 20min to Biv. Leonessa (2910m). *The bivouac hut was named after two brothers from Turin who lost their lives in mountaineering accidents, and is not a reference to an extinct lioness.*

Return to Casolari dell'Herbetet the same way.

Stage Three: descent to Valnontey (2h20min)

The royal game track (n.23) which descends here has come through the ravages of many a winter in excellent condition, and its wide, well-graded curves and built-up corners make it a delightful and relaxing walk. It snakes its way towards the valley floor, regularly visible a giddy 400m below, accompanied by swirling masses of delicately coloured butterflies attracted by the flowers. *The air is heavy with the thundering of innumerable waterfalls as they descend from the semicircle of ice masses at the head of the valley. The only unpleasant note is introduced by the small plaque in memory of a young Park ranger shot in the vicinity by poachers.*

The path turns decidedly S to avoid a steep cliff and into the welcome shade of larches, down to a bridge beneath a small waterfall, then to the nearby path junction with the main valley route where you turn left (2040m, 45min this far). (The right-hand branch leads S up to several bivouac huts as well as connecting with Alpe Money.)

Through the unusual profusion of green alder shrubs mixed with conifers, the path winds down to the bridge Ponte de l'Erfaulet (1830m, 30min) where it crosses to the right-hand side of the torrent and continues past several other path junctions and huts, widens and reaches the camping grounds and Valnontey (1666m) once more. (In ascent from Valnontey to the Casolari allow 3h.)

BIV. LEONESSA, CAI, sleeps 15 (always open)
RIF. VITTORIO SELLA tel:0165/74310. CAI, sleeps 170 (Easter-30/9)
TOURIST OFFICE COGNE tel:0165/74040

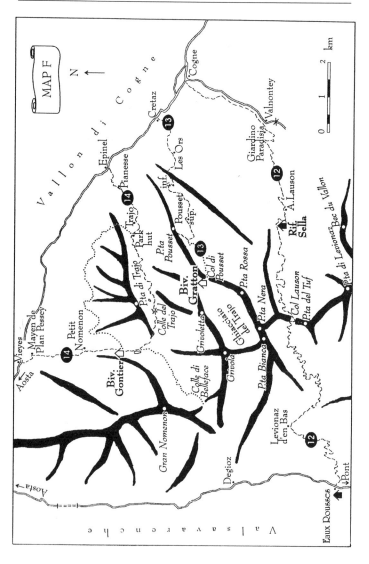

Valnontey/Valsavarenche - Col Lauson Crossing

via Valnontey - Rif. V. Sella (2h30min) - Col Lauson (2h15min) - Punta del Tuf (30min return time) - Eaux Rousses (3h30min)
Total walking time: **8h45min (2 days suggested)**

A magnificent, rewarding traverse and important segment of the Alta Via 2, despite the monumental 1600m ascent/descent involved on both sides of 3296m Col Lauson. The landscape is surprisingly varied with both woods and vast grassed and debris flanks, not to mention the sweeping panoramas. Wildlife in all shapes and sizes is equally numerous in both valleys, though on the desolate eastern flanks humans are few and far between.

The sole difficulty concerns the pass itself: the terrain in the immediate vicinity of Col Lauson is unstable and steepish. In early summer the sheltered western side is inadvisable for inexperienced walkers as it tends to be snowbound and/or icy, but by midsummer it is generally trouble-free and easily passable - check at the refuge if in doubt.

The side trip to panoramic Punta del Tuf (3393m) is only recommended in good conditions for experienced walkers.

The first stage of this walk, as far as Rif. V. Sella, is particularly suitable for family day trips - see Walk 11 for further details.

Access: There are summer buses (July to mid-September) from Cogne to the small settlement of Valnontey (SVAP company), otherwise it takes 45min on foot.

The end point Eaux Rousses (Valsavarenche) is connected by year-round (SVAP) bus to Aosta, except early June and mid-September when there may be gaps between the winter school runs and the summer 15/6-15/9 service.

Car owners can park at either Valnontey or Eaux Rousses (limited space), though it's a long way back by bus to collect your vehicle.

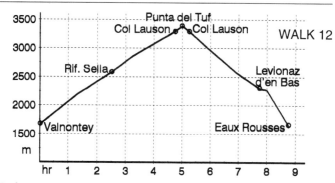

Path to Valnontey (45min)
Part of the AV2, this is a worthwhile stroll in its own right.

Shortly downhill from the main square and bus stop in Cogne (1534m), signposting (n.25) near Hotel Sant'Orso indicates the way (S) across manicured meadows, the Prati di Sant'Orso. They were named after Saint Ursus, an Irish monk who freed the valley from poisonous serpents thus enabling farmers to cultivate the land. The backdrop of glaciers ahead (SSW) belong to the Tribolazione and Roccia Viva groups. Further on over a bridge, turn left past tennis courts and bar. The pleasant path takes you along the right-hand banks of the torrent through treed and flowered clearings, to the settlement of Valnontey with its cluster of small hotels. You join the path described below just after the bridge.

Stage One: from Valnontey to Rif. V. Sella (2h30min)
From Valnontey (1666m) path n.18 (signposted for Rif. Sella) crosses the main torrent to climb (W) past the botanical garden "Giardino Paradisia" and up the mountainside following the wide easy curves of an old mule track. After the larch wood, the path crosses open terrain inhabited by numerous marmots and herds of ibex, with chamois on the slopes further away S. Close behind the old hunting lodge on the edge of the central section of the valley stands hospitable Rif. V. Sella (2584m).

See Stage One of Walk 11 for more details about the refuge and surrounding area. The notch of Col Lauson is clearly visible due W. (Timing for this stage in descent - 1h40min.)

Stage Two: ascent to Col Lauson (2h15min)

Signposted in the vicinity of the old hunting lodge, path n.18, alias Alta Via 2 (black and yellow triangle), heads W up the gentle grassed slopes on the right-hand side of the wide valley. *The gentle gradient and ample width are explained by the fact that it was another of the mid 19th century tracks the king had constructed so that the pass could be reached on horseback.* After a stretch alongside the stream, some 45min up is the turn-off (right) for Punta Rossa, but you continue left and up into a final flat upper valley. *The slopes are covered by debris, scattered with saxifrage and clumps of alpine buttercups. Ptarmigan are not unknown here, while eagles inhabit the higher reaches.*

The climb becomes decidedly stiffer and numerous zigzags cut up to a brief gully to a "false" col (not the actual pass yet), preceding a diagonal short exposed but aided passage fitted with a series of well-anchored chains, due to the crumbly nature of the terrain. The pass is only a brief curving climb away now. *Col Lauson is also called Colle Loson - closer to the origin of the name "lose", slippery black shale, which usually comes away in slabs and is used locally for roofing.* At 3296m this is the highest non-glacier pass accessible to walkers in the Park. *For Yeld and Coolidge last century it was "probably the highest path traversed by horses, and not leading over a glacier, in the Alps".* The most impressive peak back over Valnontey is Torre del Gr. S. Pietro (SE). (Reverse timing approx. 1h30min.)

Side trip to Punta del Tuf (30min return time)

For walkers with some climbing experience, the ascent of adjoining (S) Punta del Tuf (3393m) is suggested for a more vast panorama, as the view is somewhat limited from the narrow pass. In the absence of snow or ice, the peak can be reached in about 15min (same for the return) via the easy crest. The panorama takes in Punta Basei SW and Gran Sassière WSW, and M. Emilius, the Matterhorn and M. Rosa NE. The crest running SE from here to Gran Serra features an unusual series of bright to pale yellows, due to outcrops of gypsum-bearing limestones, clearly visible from Rif. Sella as well. *The name Tuf was used earlier for the whole crest, and is a reference to this calcareous rock, not volcanic origins.*

Stage Three: descent via Levionaz d'en Bas (2h30min) to Eaux Rousses (1h)

The initial part of the descent path, NNW at first, may be icy but by midsummer is usually clear and straightforward. *This ample desolate valley is characterised by vast debris slopes, which give way to meagre grass, populated by chamois, ibex and marmots further down.* A vast knoll (at approx. 3000m) some 40min down affords a glimpse S of the Gran Paradiso peak, not to mention massive M. Taou Blanc SW long visible on the opposite side of Valsavarenche.

Dazzling horizontal strata of light-grey-brown-red rock, calcareous schist for the main part, characterise the opposite flank W, an outrunner of the Grivola (N). The path winds its way almost lazily downhill, in the wide curves suitable for the king's mounted hunting parties. Soon after another prominent knoll (at approx. 2700m), carpeted with tiny bright gentians, the path heads decisively S, and the craggy snowbound pyramid of the Herbetet (*from "small pasture"*) comes into sight SSE. Soon afterwards is a signed path junction, Livionaz-Demont (2581m, about 1h40min from the pass). *The name is a reference to the highest of the three groups of old farm buildings in this valley, out of sight briefly uphill.* The turn-off (S) connects to Rif. Chabod (experienced walkers only). Instead, continuing downhill W, a watercourse is soon crossed and, high on the left-hand side of the main valley now, the path coasts above grazing flats with the ubiquitous ibex and marmots. Shrub vegetation including some alpenrose has begun to colonise the valley here.

A brief climb leads to several old farm buildings, now converted into Park premises, known as Levionaz d'en Bas, or Livionaz-Desot (2303m), the lowest of the three groups. Drinking water is available. (50min from the signed junction).

On the lower edge of the Levionaz valley now, the Valsavarenche floor starts to come into view, and is just over 1h away. Heading left (S) the path moves into the shade of a beautiful larch and Arolla pine wood. *It is alive with squirrels and noisy speckled nutcrackers on their late summer food-gathering excursions, while the undergrowth is bright red with cow- and bearberry shrubs.* On a long level section the path never seems to make up its mind whether or not to actually descend until a watercourse is crossed. The final stretch above the hamlet is swept by avalanches in winter, as testified by a sizeable debris fan scattered with broken trees. A walled-in path through the fields takes you via the bridge across the Torrent Savara to Eaux Rousses (1666m), a cluster of old stone buildings, including the carefully restored upmarket guesthouse Hostellerie du Paradis, which has an annex-cum-dormitory for walkers (*half board is compulsory but reasonable, and hot showers are included*).

Note: the nearest food shops are 4km downhill at Degioz, or 5km uphill at Pont.

The name Eaux Rousses refers to the red rock behind the hamlet, stained by the water that trickles down from a ferruginous spring.

(Reverse timing for this stage is some 5h in ascent to Col Lauson - only recommended for those with sufficient stamina to face the colossal 1600m climb.)

RIF. VITTORIO SELLA tel:0165/74310 CAI, sleeps 170 (Easter-30/9)
HOSTELLERIE DU PARADIS (Eaux Rousses) tel:0165/905972 Private hotel with a "Foresteria" ie. dormitory. Sleeps 22 (open year-round).
TOURIST OFFICE COGNE tel:0165/74040
TOURIST OFFICE DEGIOZ (Valsavarenche) tel:0165/905816 (seasonal)

WALK 13 *(see map F, p.86)*

Vallon di Cogne - The Local "Gornergrat"

---

via Cretaz - Pousset Superiore (3h) - Punta Pousset (1h30min) - return to Cretaz (3h)
Total walking time: **7h30min (1 day)**

The name for extraordinarily panoramic 3046m Punta Pousset comes from the French "poucet" meaning thumb, due to its resemblance to an upright thumb, visible from many points in the Cogne valley Perhaps the first mountaineers to record their visit, Yeld and Coolidge writing in 1893 called it "the Gornergrat of Cogne". The wide-ranging views are unbeatable, but there the resemblance to the Swiss peak ends, luckily, as neither the cogwheel train nor the floods of tourists is to be found here.

Punta Pousset, and the hefty 1500m climb involved, is well

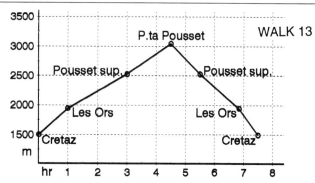

known amongst the locals, though the only frequenters likely to be encountered in large numbers will be the wildlife - sizeable herds of chamois as well as ibex in the upper reaches of Vallone del Pousset.

Nothing more than a reasonable dose of stamina, healthy quadriceps muscles, and a good picnic lunch is required, as the itinerary is within reach of average walkers. Weather-wise, a perfect, cloudless day is recommended.

Experienced walkers (only) can extend the walk by returning via Col di Pousset.

Access: Cretaz, 1.5km before Cogne, is on the year-round bus line (SVAP) from Aosta. Car parking is possible in the village centre.

Stage One: via Les Ors (1h) and Pousset superiori (2h) to Punta Pousset (1h30min)

Make an early start from Cretaz (1499m). Head across the two watercourses, and take the marked path (n.26) that climbs W through wood and pasture to the group of huts known as Les Ors (1944m). Soon at a signed path junction, take the right branch onto the ridge which separates the Vallone di Vermiana and Vallone del Pousset. You climb past a Park warden's hut (1h from Les Ors) then down to cross the stream near the Pousset inferiori huts (2179m). The path continues W alongside the stream and crosses it again before climbing up to a vast area of glacially polished rock. Not far on you reach the old Pousset superiori huts (2529m, 3h this far).

Keep on (right) above the huts and proceed over a series of grassy terraces, where herds of chamois graze. At the next marked junction (approx. 2800m), take the right branch (left proceeds to Col di Pousset and Biv. Gratton). It curves its way northish, cutting across the steep grassy flank at the head of the valley. You eventually emerge on the crest, briefly W of the peak, where an easy clamber is all that separates you from the rocky point of Punta Pousset (3046m) and a breathtaking panorama. As Yeld and Coolidge put it, "Cogne is at your feet", not to mention what appears to be the whole of the Alps as well.

Extension via Col di Pousset

It is possible - with experience, a head for heights and a good couple of hours to spare - to connect with Col di Pousset, SW. You follow the rocky crest back and round another rocky turret (3058m), keeping to its right. The spectacular pass over the Ghiacciaio del Trajo, N of Punta Rossa, is also the site of Biv. Gratton (3198m). *This unmanned bivouac hut was set up in 1985 by the Cogne Alpine Guides Association as a staging point during the ascent of the Grivola. It is always open, however intending users will need to be fully equipped.*

From the pass and hut, head down ENE to the junction above the Pousset superiori huts where you join the main itinerary.

Stage Two: descent to Cretaz (3h)

Return the same way.

BIV. GRATTON Private, sleeps 9, always open
TOURIST OFFICE COGNE tel:0165/74040

WALK 14 *(see map F, p.86)*

Vallon di Cogne -
The Eagle, the Ibex and the Maiden

---

via Epinel - Trajo (1h30min) - Park hut (20min) - Colle del Trajo (2h10min) - Biv. Gontier (1h) - [Alt. traverse to Biv. Gontier (3h)] - Vieyes (2h)
Total walking time: **7h (1-2 days suggested)**

The centrepiece of this unfrequented loop route is a "beautiful maiden", the Grivola, a magnificent pointed 3969m peak, first scaled in 1859 by a group of British climbers and a local game warden. The best Grivola viewing point is the Alpe Gran Nomenon, site of Biv. Gontier, in the second part of the itinerary. Second-in-line in magnificence, if not fame, is the elegant Gran Nomenon, which towers over the valley of the same name. For the geologically minded, the Grivola is composed of calcareous schist with ophiolites, in contrast to the metadiorites that make up the Gran Nomenon.

The walk includes long climbs and descents, often on rugged terrain, and rates average on the difficulty scale. All effort is amply rewarded by the superb views together with the excellent chance of observing sizeable herds of chamois and ibex at close quarters, along with birds of prey. The ibex tend to stay put on the path even at the approach of walkers, so you won't come far from bumping into one at times. An encounter with the giant "ibex king", however, is the stuff of legends. Renowned as a sort of devil who uttered strange languages and carried off children, his reputation was enhanced after a challenge from the valley's fearless "hunter king". The encounter was brief as the hunter, blinded by false superiority, was sent hurtling down a ravine.

In contrast, humanitarian qualities were attributed to a gigantic golden eagle, erstwhile resident of the Grivola peak. A very ancient legend recounts how the local people, tired of suffering intense cold and mists, turned to the eagle for help. With his blazing eyes he set dead trees alight, and thus introduced man to fire and heat.

Note: the Alternative traverse given involves several exposed passages, and the path is not in very good condition. On the other hand the desolate northern flanks of Punta di Trajo offer more views over the Vallon di Cogne, wildlife in the form of countless ibex and probably no other walkers. It could also be used as an alternative return route from Biv. Gontier to the Trajo valley, thus a ring walk which returns to Epinel.

In any case an overnight stay at the comfortable stone and timber chalet Biv. Gontier is highly recommended. A converted shepherd's hut, unmanned but well equipped for both cooking and sleeping, it is anything but "unalluring" as Yeld and Coolidge described the then available huts a century ago, though they did

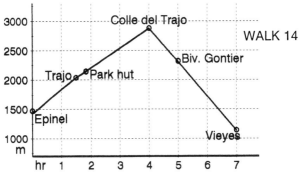

make a special mention of the "unrivalled position". The hut is normally locked, but a phone call to book a bed, and stop-off in Aymavilles at the start of Vallon di Cogne to collect the keys, are all that's needed. A donation towards upkeep can be left in the hut.

Access: Both Epinel and Vieyes are served by the year-round Aosta to Cogne (SVAP) bus line, and are 3.5km and 10km respectively from Cogne. Those with a car can park in either village, and return by bus.

Stage One: ascent via Trajo (1h30min) to Park hut (20min)

From Epinel (1470m) take the wide bridge across Torrente Grand'Eyvia. There is signposting for path n.27, an unremitting climb SW winding beneath lovely conifers, whose needles make the going soft underfoot. It's a good 45min to the arrival point of a mechanised cableway and huts, Pianesse (1743m). Keep left and up diagonally and the path soon emerges onto an open slope, to bear right across a rubble gully in the shade of Punta Pousset (S), with promising glimpses of the upper valley. A stretch of wood, mostly larch, and several stream crossings on is the turn-off for Trajo (2037m). A minute away over the rise is the picturesque cluster of stone-slab roofed houses, built in timber that has weathered to a rich red-brown. Inhabited now exclusively by marmots and mice, they look NE to M. Emilius. *Depending on the map, the name is also spelt Trajoz or Traso, the closest to the local pronunciation. The name was probably taken from the Colle, and refers to a route followed by shepherds with their livestock.*

95

Back on the main path, keep climbing to the Park warden's hut, set in a panoramic clearing at 2150m. (1h15min is sufficient for this stage in descent.)

Stage Two: via Colle del Trajo (2h10min) to Biv. Gontier (1h)

N.27 proceeds essentially W and out of the trees, climbing around an old moraine ridge which descends from the diminutive Grivoletta glacier. Soon a steep rocky flank and unusual yellowish rock gully require some effort. This climb is somewhat deceptive as the actual pass is expected at its end. However you emerge onto a flattish pasture basin housing a small lake, where herds of chamois are a frequent sight. The Colle del Trajo is that higher pass ahead (W), but it's not as steep going now. Early and late summer walkers should expect some snow.

Once at Colle del Trajo (2877m), you're between Punta Crevasse (S) and Punta di Trajo (N), but it is of course the Grivola that demands attention. (1h30min for this section in the opposite direction.)

The descent is generally problem-free and zigzags due W at first down another stony slope. This terminates in a further level basin with yet more chamois, in Vallone di Gran Nomenon now. An easy stretch N above the torrent leads to the final brief descent to the Alpe Gran Nomenon cluster of huts including another National Park ranger's summer residence. Welcoming Biv. Gontier (2315m) is the separate modernised chalet.

Here the imposing pyramid of the Grivola (due S now) can be enjoyed from another viewpoint, together with its sister Gran Nomenon SW, not to mention the wide-ranging views N to the snowcapped ridges beyond Aosta.

(Allow 1h30min from Biv. Gontier to Colle del Trajo in ascent.)

Alternative: traverse from Park hut to Biv. Gontier (3h)

This path actually skirts the midriff of Punta di Trajo, and was the work of Park rangers. Near the hut, "n.28" is painted on a rock, though old red and white marking and n.111 is often a useful guide during the traverse. A clear path turns off down right to a small stream crossing. N now, you climb the easy rock face up among pines. There are views back towards the Grivoletta (SW) and small

Bivacco Gontier

glaciers.

After rounding the flank, an exposed stretch follows, necessitating a sure foot and clear head. You have now swung around to overlook the main valley and Epinel. The terrain alternates between fallen rock and shrub-grass cover, in combination with some superb specimens of weather-beaten Arolla pines.

A first wide side valley is crossed without difficulty, the up-down rhythm of the path a regular feature by now. *It will already be clear from the veritable mountains of droppings covering the path that this is the reign of ibex and chamois rather than humans.* Just under midway, the second valley to be crossed is in very bad condition and you spend time scrambling over land- and rockslips. Even though the path has disappeared in places, the direction is no problem as the path ahead is continually visible. As you climb out of this valley too there is a longish cliff-hugging stretch. Once the sign "Pericolo" - Danger - is behind you it is easier going.

Following a third and easier final valley, you swing left (S) to enter the Vallone di Gran Nomenon, to be rewarded with wide-ranging views. As the path skirts the rocky flanks high above the cows at pasture and the shepherds' huts dotted over the slopes below, a little extra care is also recommended for the narrow stretches. Grass is finally reached and a slab-rock bridge leads to Biv. Gontier and a relax. (Timing is the same in the opposite direction.)

Extension to Colle di Belleface (4h return time)
From Biv. Gontier, over a brief rise, the path, in common with that from Colle del Trajo, runs the entire length of the grassy basin in a southerly direction. It then bears SW and becomes fainter. Steep and tiring at times, it ascends the valley amongst fallen rocks, and you are left to your own devices when the path disappears. 2h30min should suffice to Colle di Belleface (3009m), between the Grivola and Gran Nomenon peaks, an awesome position. *The name evidently means a steep sunny pasture area for goats.*
Note: the idea of traversing to neighbouring Valsavarenche might seem appealing, however at the time of writing long sections of the old royal game track in descent to Degioz were reported to be in a bad state.

Stage Three: descent to Vieyes (2h)
Yellow arrows for n.5 wander across the hillside northwards. You cross to the right-hand side of the stream to drop past the Petit Nomenon shepherds' huts (2191m). Soon in a wood of silver fur, where cushions of the rare twinflower are said to grow, it winds pleasantly downwards. It eventually crosses back left beneath an impressive waterfall in a narrow section of valley, laden thickets of raspberries lining the path.

The next significant landmark is the Mayen de Plan Pessey (1361m), traditionally a medium-altitude farm for early grazing, "Mayen" referring to May. Go diagonally left now into the particularly tall and thick wood. The path curves easily down along old stone terracing on the final stretch, and comes out on the road near a bus stop.

Just across the road is the quiet village of Vieyes (1142m), whose few remaining inhabitants desert it during the sunless winter months. Apart from drinking water, a public phone and a bench, it offers visitors a small frescoed church.

(Reverse timing: allow 4h. While easy, it is a little monotonous in ascent as there are no views until the valley opens out on the very last leg.)

BIV. M. GONTIER Private, sleeps 16. Keys from Elio Gontier (Aymavilles) tel:0165/902259, or Fulvio Gorrex (Aymavilles) tel:0165/902738. Equipped with blankets, wood stove, cooking gear. Water nearby.
TOURIST OFFICE COGNE tel:0165/74040 tel:0165/74040

WALK 15 *(see map G, p.100)*
Vallon di Cogne - Pondel's Roman Bridge

---

via bus stop (for Pondel) - Roman bridge (15min) - traverse via Issogne to Aymavilles (1h15min)
Total walking time: **1h30min** ($^{1}/_{2}$ day)

The great attraction of this fascinating itinerary is a marvellous and intact, two-storeyed Roman bridge. It was built in 3 BC to carry the unusual combination of water, people and goods across a deep gorge. A toll was charged for pedestrians and livestock who used the covered lower passage, while the top level constituted the aqueduct. The water was channelled down the westernmost bank of the Torrente Grand Eyvia from Chevril, some 3km up the valley towards Cogne. Traces of the excavated channels, originally 1-1$^{1}/_{2}$m wide and 1$^{1}/_{2}$-2m deep, are still visible along the rock face, though external suspended passages have disappeared. The supply was destined for Roman settlements on the lower western flanks facing the main Aosta valley, probably for both agriculture and sand quarrying, but local stories tell of a gold mine as well. The bridge was a mere "branch" from this main channel across to Pondel, once an important Roman stronghold against the local Salasso population who were holding out further up the Cogne valley.

According to the inscription on the keystone, Aimus and Avilius, two settlers from Padua, or Roman consuls in another version, had the bridge built at their own expense, and also gave their names to the nearby village of Aymavilles.

Apart from the compulsory visit to the actual bridge, the walk

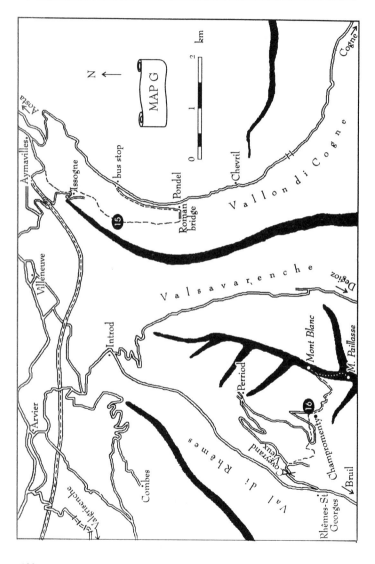

described is a novel way of returning to Aymavilles.
Note: a torch is handy for the brief tunnel encountered in Stage Two. You traverse to the minuscule hamlet of Issogne, not to be confused with the township and castle of Issogne, in eastern Valle d'Aosta.
Access: the Aosta-Cogne bus (SVAP) will let you off at the Pondel turn-off, about 4km from Aymavilles. By car you can drive all the way to the village of Pondel, but those intending to do the complete walk would be better off leaving their vehicle in Aymavilles.

Stage One: to Pondel and the bridge-cum-aqueduct (15min)

From the signposted turn-off for Pondel, it's a quiet walk down to the hamlet (890m), also referred to as Pont d'Ael. *Experts say this is incorrect as the name is derived from "ponticulus", small bridge.* Arrows guide visitors through the maze of houses to the astounding 50.5m long, 2.20m wide bridge, spanning the torrent at a height of 61.5m. Once you've crossed the bridge, the interior can also be explored by way of side entrances.

Stage Two: via Issogne (50min) to Aymavilles (25min)

Take path n.2 (yellow signposting) along N, high above the torrent. It follows abandoned stone terracing which once supported vineyards and orchards. The hot dry terrain is the domain now of crickets and butterflies. As well as interesting snowcapped ridges visible NE beyond Aosta, there are good views back of the bridge, backed by the distant Grivola and a glimpse of glaciers.

After some 15min of gradual ascent and clear yellow arrow markings, the path branches up left diagonally heading for a seemingly impassable rock barrier. Here, surprisingly enough, you encounter a 60m-long tunnel excavated in the rock by First World War Austrian POWs, who

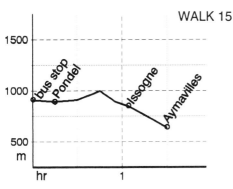

101

are also to be thanked for the Cogne road. While it has one "window", a torch is handy.

The path now zigzags down the steep flank then resumes its N direction, and feels a little exposed for a brief stretch. Crumbly side gullies are crossed with wood bridges, and chamois may be surprised in the mixed wood. After skirting a vineyard and crossing a torrent, the path emerges alongside the apple and pear orchard belonging to a very old rambling farmhouse, Issogne.

Take the surfaced road down right through masses of late summer blackberries. Waymarking for the old path points off right where you drop quickly between old walls and a thick chestnut wood with scavenging squirrels and noisy black grouse. Foxes and wild boar are not unknown here either. As you round the hillside on the edge of the main Aosta valley, the fanciful turrets of the 11th century castle of St. Pierre appear ahead. Down through the manicured vineyards of Aymavilles, you emerge onto a narrow surfaced road (where signposting for path n.2 gives reverse timing from here as 1h30min). Once over the bridge there are apple and pear orchards as well as houses at Moulins, then you bear right and soon reach the main square of Aymavilles (641m). *As well as shops, bars and the like, there is a modest villa-cum-castle, and the Church of Saint-Léger (uphill right), with an unusual 18th century trompe l'oeil frescoed façade.*

TOURIST OFFICE AYMAVILLES tel:0165/902693 (seasonal)

WALK 16 *(see map G, p.100)*
Val di Rhêmes - 2205m Mont Blanc

---

via Rhêmes-Saint-Georges - Champromenty (1h45min) - Mont Blanc (1h) - Champromenty (40min) - Rhêmes-Saint-Georges (1h15min)
Total walking time: **4h40min (1 day)**

A well-kept local secret, this modest (2205m) Mont Blanc is easily "scaled" without ice-axe or crampons. Its isolated and commanding position at the start of Val di Rhêmes give it sweeping, virtually uninterrupted views over the Valle d'Aosta taking in the spectacular (4810m) Mont Blanc to Grandes Jorasses line-up, the Grand Combin, the Grivola and Gran Paradiso, to mention but a few. It owes its name to the light colour of its calcareous rock. Walkers can generally count on the access tracks being clear as early as May and as late as November due to its extended exposure to the sun. The first stretch is an easy path which becomes a wide dirt track, making it feasible for anyone who can manage the climb of 1000m. Added attractions are the stable colony of ibex around the peak and a good chance of sighting chamois in the woods.

The nearest accommodation is further upvalley towards Rhêmes-Notre-Dame.

Access: Rhêmes-Saint-Georges in the Val di Rhêmes is connected by year-round, if infrequent, bus from Aosta (SAVDA).

By car you can drive as far as Coveyrand-Vieux.

Stage One: via Coveyrand-Vieux (15min) then Champromenty (1h30min) to Mont Blanc (1h)

A short distance uphill from the bus stop and lone shop at Rhêmes-Saint-Georges (1159m), take the turn-off signposted for Coveyrand-Vieux. The narrow asphalt road climbs N past houses and, a little over 1km up, reaches the Ecole Maternelle in a small square and parking area (1234m). *The bells of the nearby church were commandeered by the French in 1800 to be converted into cannons.*

Path n.301 heads uphill (E) on the narrow road which soon

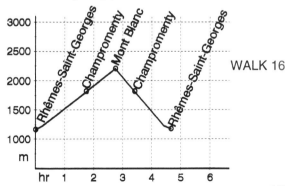

becomes a dirt track, and is closed to unauthorised traffic. After 10min you turn right at a prominent fork, even though Champromenty and Mont Blanc are signposted to the left (via the road, a much lengthier variant). A path (n.301) branches left off this track straight away. Follow it through light vegetation and left again across a stream. It cuts up through the wood climbing steadily, with regular yellow and red paint marking. You intersect the road at approx. 1550m then again at 1690m, before emerging from the bird-filled conifer forest to join the road on the final stretch to the picturesque summer farm, Mayen de Champromenty (1813m), complete with characteristic stone-slab roof, turret and drinking water. *The designation in dialect "mayen" means a medium-altitude farm that can be utilised as early as May (hence the name) to provide the livestock with fresh grass while waiting for the snow to melt on the higher altitude pastures (where the huts are known as "montagnes").*

No-one can expect shepherds to live in uninteresting places, and in fact the outlook here is simply wonderful: though limited to the Val di Rhêmes, it takes in pointed Becca di Tey (SSW) and the Grande Rousse to its immediate S and the rest of the ridge.

Continue up the wide track E at first, then moving around N. *There are thick banks of pink alpenrose beneath thinning larch, a meagre cover for the shy chamois who usually betray their presence by dislodging stones.* The views open up gradually, as you head in the direction of a modest mount due N, recognisable for its distinctive light colour. At the wide saddle of Col du Mont Blanc (2170m, Park noticeboard) leave the track and head for the Park hut. Just before it, take the path left around the rocky outcrop where a sizeable herd of ibex regularly sojourns. A grassy slope, then a scramble and you are on the highest point of breathtaking Mont Blanc (2205m). The view ranges virtually uninterrupted from W to ENE (Mont Blanc NW) then resumes SE with the slender sharp points of the Gran Nomenon and Grivola, followed by Gran Paradiso and Ciarfaron to the S.

Extension to M. Paillasse (1h15min return time): for those with extra energy to burn, an even more extensive outlook, especially E, can be gained in exchange for a further 40min (or 250m) in ascent. From the saddle Col du Mont Blanc, rejoin the track and proceed S along the wide grassy ridge then wide curves up to 2414m and the top of M. Paillasse and its trig point.

Stage Two: return via Champromenty (40min) to Coveyrand-Vieux (1h) and Rhêmes-Saint-Georges (15min)
Return the same way. From Champromenty, however, you can follow the road down. It makes for a more leisurely descent, but be warned: it is a lot longer.

TOURIST OFFICE BRUIL (Rhêmes-Notre-Dame) tel:0165/96114 (seasonal)

WALK 17 *(see map H, p.106)*
Valsavarenche - Below the Gran Paradiso

---

via Pravieux - Rif. Chabod (2h30min) - Rif. Vittorio Emanuele II (2h) - Pont (1h30min)
Total walking time: **6h (1-2 days suggested)**

Yet another excellent route including a superb high altitude traverse with sweeping panoramas, connecting two important and popular refuges, both essential bases for mountaineers heading for the Gran Paradiso peak. At 4061m and the only peak wholly within Italian territory that exceeds 4000m, it was first scaled by English climbers J.J. Cowell and W. Dundas in 1860 with two French guides, Michel Payot and Jean Tairraz.

This popular ascent signifies that an overnight stay in these huts usually includes being woken at an ungodly hour as groups set out for the summit. Of the two huts, modern Rif. Chabod is probably quieter and more comfortable. Advance booking is strongly recommended for both refuges, especially midsummer, and weekends are to be avoided if possible. **Note:** Multilingual signs at Pont advise visitors that police regulations do not allow Rif. Vittorio Emanuele II to accept more people than it can accommodate. A guesthouse at Pont is listed as an alternative, and there is a large camping ground also.

This is one of the best walks for families as it is problem free, as

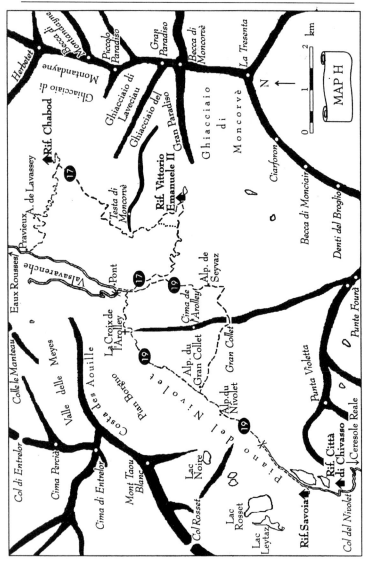

long as the length and climbs are taken into account. Trying to fit it into a single day means a rather long haul. Plenty of wild animals, especially ibex, are easily seen along the way, usually grazing or involved in mock battles.

The route can of course be followed in the opposite direction, and the appropriate timing is given. The most popular section is the Pont-Rif. Vittorio Emanuele II path, less varied than the Rif. Chabod ascent, while the traverse is relatively untrodden.

Access: Valsavarenche is served by (SAVDA) buses from Aosta all year round as far as Eaux Rousses, but there may be gaps early June and late September between the winter school runs and the summer (15/6-15/9) service, which extends as far as Pont several times a day.

Pravieux, where the walk starts, is approx. 3km downhill from Pont and 2km uphill from Eaux Rousses, and buses will drop you off there on request.

Drivers can leave their cars either at the parking area at Pravieux, or at the huge car park at the end of the road at Pont.

Stage One: ascent to Rif. Chabod (2h30min)

From Pravieux (Old Meadows, 1871m), follow the clear signpost for Rif. Chabod, path n.5 over the wide bridge and essentially E. You pass close to the rear of characteristic vaulted farm buildings, and a masterpiece of alpine path construction awaits you. There are carefully built-up corners on the regular curves, which keep to the left of a cascade, out of sight. *Livestock have been escorted to summer*

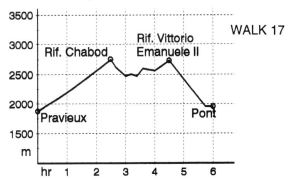

pastures along this route for centuries. *The conifer wood is alive with squirrels, nutcrackers and even the occasional lone male chamois.*

Some 1h up at 2194m is a clearing with the modest farm Alpe de Lavassey. There are ample views of the opposite flanks of Valsavarenche, even right up to Punta Basei (SW).

Keep right at the path junction (n.5A heads off to Biv. Sberna) and as the larch trees thin, immense expanses of glacially smoothed rock come into sight, often with ibex sentinels on the crests. Fawn-coated chamois graze on the grass flats, ready to flee at any hint of danger.

After a good 2h total winding and plodding above the tree line, you pass a wooden bridge (n.1A turns off S for the traverse) and shortly afterwards is the refuge's turbine (guaranteed low cost power supply) at the base of a cascade. A wide path climbs diagonally left up the final 100m to a platform and Rif. Chabod (2750m). It occupies a simply magnificent position facing the northwestern flank of the Gran Paradiso (SSE), Piccolo Paradiso, then the Becca di Montandayne (SE) which dominates the building. *The modern but simple refuge was named after a local inhabitant who became the first President of the Valle d'Aosta's autonomous government following the second world war. Hours can be spent just observing the large herds of ibex that haunt the rock slabs on the opposite bank of the torrent.*

(Reverse timing - allow 1h30min in descent.)

Stage Two: traverse to Rif. Vittorio Emanuele II (2h)

Waymarking is regular - either yellow stripes or stone cairns. The path is problem-free under normal conditions and there are no exposed stretches.

Return to the wooden bridge (10min) passed during the ascent, and once across it the path (n.1a - also Alta Via 4 waymarking) descends gradually SW. Several moraines are touched on, including a sort of funnel formed by lateral moraine ridges below the retreating blue ice belonging to the Laveciau glacier. *The name is derived from dialect word meaning a place where salt was left for ibex and chamois to lick.* After a second wooden bridge (20min on) over a tumultuous cold stream, there is a series of ups and downs as you round the Testa di Montcorvè. After a shoulder, a desolate stone-filled valley is crossed. *If you look upwards every now and again, you'll catch out ibex youngsters on high rock perches peering down.*

Back on grass once more, at a path junction (1h30min total) the refuge is visible so it seems logical to take the left branch for the final climb. (The wider track which continues straight ahead, S, eventually joins the main descent path.) Smoothed rock slabs are climbed over, and the path traverses meagre pastures populated with ibex that ignore walkers. A wooden bridge over a further ice-melt torrent, then keep left at the final path junction. *The lightly grassed terrain features gentians and oxe-eye daisies.*

Rif. Vittorio Emanuele II (2732m) stands just back from the shore of a small tarn, Moncorvè. The position is superb, even without a view of the actual peak of the Gran Paradiso (E), but that can be remedied by a brief excursion up the moraine slopes. Then virtually due S is slender pointed Becca di Monciair, while SE is the rounded form of La Tresenta and the impressive north wall of the Ciarforon is SSE.

Note: The water here is not suitable for drinking purposes.

The original refuge, the small hut still used as an annex, was inaugurated in 1884 in honour of the Hunter King and at the cost of 6160 lire. Writing in 1893, Yeld and Coolidge described it as "very commodious (5 rooms) and very well fitted up in all respects, so that it is probably the best Club hut in the Western Alps, and has therefore been named 'The Palace'". The popularity of the zone and the Gran Paradiso ascent made a more spacious building necessary, and though the decision was taken in 1927, the work was not completed until 1961 (better late than never). The strange curved metallic building is rather incongruous, however some consider it a perfect fit for these morainic surroundings.

With the aid of binoculars numbers of reclining ibex will be seen on any of the surrounding ridges, while chamois graze on the lower reaches and keep their distance. The alpine choughs can virtually be hand fed.

(Reverse timing for the traverse - 2h.)

Stage Three: descent to Pont (1h30min)
Late afternoon will guarantee an encounter with the laden pack mules necessary for supplementing the refuge's start-of-season helicopter drop of foodstuffs.

The clear well-trodden track (n.1) heads W downhill. After the initial debris-covered flanks, grass and earth reappear, but it is the ubiquitous glacially smoothed and lichen-stained slabs that dominate. The easy path means you have time to enjoy the vast landscape and views over Valsavarenche.

After endless curves the path enters larch wood with bilberries and alpenrose as undergrowth. Once down on the actual valley floor in the vicinity of an old vaulted hut and close to the torrent, it's a final 15min N along to the bridge crossing for Pont (1960m) and the enormous car park, camping ground, shop, as well as a couple of hotels and restaurants scattered down the road.

(Allow 2h for this stage in ascent.)

RIF. FEDERICO CHABOD tel:0165/95574. Private, sleeps 107 (1/7-15/9)
RIF. VITTORIO EMANUELE II tel:0165/95920. CAI, sleeps 130 (Easter-20/9)
HOTEL FIOR DI ROCCIA (Pont) tel:0165/95478 (20/6-20/9)
TOURIST OFFICE DEGIOZ tel:0165/905816 (seasonal)

WALK 18 *(see map L, p.150)*

Valsavarenche -
The King's Path in Valle delle Meyes

---

via Pont - Valle delle Meyes (2h10min) - La Croix de l'Arolley (1h40min) - Pont (40min)
Total walking time: **4h30min (1 day suggested)**

After the ascent to the solitary Valle delle Meyes, where marmot, ibex and eagle viewings are guaranteed, the itinerary heads S along one of the best preserved and the most panoramic stretches of royal game track in this northern section of the Park. It affords a magnificent sweeping panorama over Valsavarenche to the Gran Paradiso group of peaks in their snow and ice setting. No particular difficulty is involved, and it is perfectly suitable for energetic family groups.

This route also lends itself to several excellent variations: it can form a link with Walk 26 north via Colle le Manteau then Lac Djouan

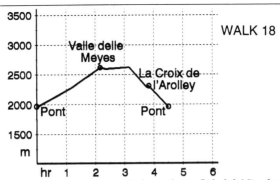

to Eaux Rousses, or can be extended south to Col del Nivolet. Timing is given at the appropriate points.

Access: see Walk 17.

Stage One: ascent from Pont to Valle delle Meyes junction (2h10min)

At Pont (1960m), a short distance downhill from the main car park, next to the Genzianella Hotel, is the start of a wide track. *It was to have been an access road over S to the Col del Nivolet for the purposes of a late '60s mammoth hydroelectric project which never materialised.* This initial 3km stretch (marked n.4), totally abandoned nowadays, constitutes a convenient and panoramic access for the Valle delle Meyes, and though it is obviously closed to 4-wheeled traffic, it is popular with mountain bikers. After several wide curves, it heads decisively N and, 30min on, includes a short tunnel (torch not necessary). Just as the second tunnel is reached a further 30min up, as the road turns left, take the path off straight ahead (faint n.4 marking). Ignore the yellow arrows for a mountain bike itinerary, and head up diagonally left on the upper branch. Ten minutes will see you at a shrine near old farm huts (Meyes di sotto, 2275m - incorrectly positioned on the IGC map). The view E across the valley to the Gran Paradiso and surrounding peaks and glaciers is nothing less than breathtaking, but it improves. *Quiet walkers have a good chance of watching chamois at relatively close quarters in this area.*

The path is wider now and, in combination with a route which started out from Ponte del Gran Clapey (1727m), heads SW in wide curves and soon climbs to a picturesque huddle of huts (Meyes di

111

Picturesque huts, Meyes di sopra

sopra, 2518m) which blends in perfectly with its rock-lichen surroundings.

Not much further up and a final series of ex-glacial "steps" gives access to the central section of Valle delle Meyes, where your passage will undoubtedly send marmots shrieking and scampering in all directions. After a small lake is a signposted path junction (2615m) as you join the wide ex-hunting track in this desolate and unfrequented valley. Views onto the Gran Paradiso group are partially obscured from here, but better viewing spots are reached in all directions.

(Allow 1h30min in descent for this stage.)

With time to spare it is worthwhile continuing W up Valle delle Meyes for further exploration. The narrow path crosses moraine and ventures to the foot of small Ghiacciaio di Percià. *Eagle sightings are not unusual in these upper reaches. The raptors are said to have perfected the hunting technique of knocking wild animals off their rock crest lookout positions.*

Link with Colle le Manteau (45min) then Lac Djouan (45min)

Take the wide track (n.9) heading N (right branch). Once on the actual southern flank of the Costa le Manteau, the old version of which was "le Mentò", it climbs in easy wide curves, giving you ample time to observe the ibex grazing or at rest among the scattered rocks.

The ample panoramic crest is crossed at 2795m at Colle le Manteau (not usually named on maps). The outlook is quite incredible.

The track in descent NW to Lac Djouan, visible below, was reconstructed in 1964, and like the southern side, is a long easy series of bends. Down in the valley it merges into the main path from Col di Entrelor, where you turn down right (NE) towards the lake. See Walk 26, Stage 0ne from here on.

(In the opposite direction, allow 1h for the ascent from Lac Djouan to Colle le Manteau, and 20min to the Valle delle Meyes junction.)

Stage Two: traverse to Pian Borgno junction (1h)
From the Valle delle Meyes path junction, turn left on n.9 heading first E then S. Gradual descent leads through squelchy boggy flats alongside the stream. Both waymarking and path tend to peter out periodically then reappear. Your aim is to cross the watercourse and rejoin the wide stretch of track visible ahead SE in order to round the rock bastion of the Costa des Aouille - the name probably comes from eagle. Just past the corner is a lookout point par excellence: high over deep U-shaped Valsavarenche is an imposing ridge running S then SW, featuring from left to right, the Herbetet, Becca di Montandayne, Piccolo and Gran Paradiso, Tresenta, Ciarforon, Becca di Monciair and Denti del Broglio.

The path continues its gradual climb as it enters Pian Borgno, another high altitude marshy flat soaked by several meltwater streams from higher glacier pockets glimpsed around M. Taou Blanc (SW, the name refers to the whitish-yellow rock). It's worth checking the rocks up right every now and again for chamois. A small tarn precedes a stream crossing on stepping stones. Not far around now, orderly mounds of stones left after pasture clearing work announce a path junction and faded signpost, at 2620m.

(Just under 1h is sufficient for this stage in the opposite direction.)

Extension to Col del Nivolet (2h)

N.2A continues straight on (SSW) for the Col del Nivolet and road pass - see Walk 19 for accommodation and access information.

Stage Three: descent via La Croix de l'Arolley (40min) to Pont (40min)

For the descent towards La Croix de l'Arolley hence Pont, take the left turning (n.3A), decisively downhill. Another excellent easy well-kept path, it winds valleywards between curious dry stone columns cum oversized cairns. Flights of stone steps lead quickly to the dirt road at 2485m, a surviving stretch of the Pont-Col del Nivolet road project. You cut straight across it - signposted n.3 for Pont. Continue down to the abandoned huts of Alp. de Turin (2388m), but before actually reaching them, take the unnumbered path off left (ignore n.3A which turns right). In the vicinity of cascades, it crosses a clearing with profusions of spotted gentians beneath power lines and across a wooden bridge. The main Pont-Col del Nivolet track (n.3) is joined not far from an old wooden cross in a commanding position. A well used local reference point, La Croix de l'Arolley or Croce Arolley (2310m) derives its name from the Arolla pine.

From here the path drops down E in a series of tight zigzags, with built-up corners, well reinforced, and in the proximity of a waterfall (left) enters a larch wood with alpenrose and juniper shrubs. Not far above the road, a fork off right leads to the Pont car park and camping area, otherwise keeping straight on you emerge on the road, only a couple of metres uphill from the starting point.

(In ascent from Pont to La Croix allow 1h, then 2h for the remaining distance to the Pian Borgno junction.)

HOTEL FIOR DI ROCCIA (Pont) tel:0165/95478 (20/6-20/9)
TOURIST OFFICE DEGIOZ tel:0165/905816 (seasonal)

WALK 19 *(see map H, p.106)*
Valsavarenche/Piano del Nivolet - A Sea of White Ranunculus

via Pont - Gran Collet (2h30min) - Alp. du Gran Collet (40min) [direct route from Pont via La Croix de l'Arolley (1h40min)] - Col del Nivolet (1h40min)
Total walking time: **4h50min [direct route 3h20min] (1 day suggested)**

The main itinerary climbs steeply and quickly to the spectacular Gran Collet pass, a fascinating, if long way to enter the Piano del Nivolet. This vast altopiano 2300-2500m above sea level is famous for its unrivalled spectacle in early summer when it is transformed into a sea of white by the blooms of the buttercup *Ranunculus pyrenaeus*. At the southernmost extremity is the Col del Nivolet road pass and access to the southern Piedmont side of the Park, meaning dramatic contrasts in landscape.

This Gran Collet route is less popular than others in Valsavarenche and care should be taken not to disturb the large herds of both chamois and ibex with their young in the upper reaches of the valley to be climbed. As far as views go, it is incomparable, thanks to the proximity of the Gran Paradiso and its entourage.

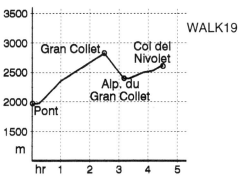

115

While the walk is not particularly difficult, the climb is steep and relentless, requiring a good dose of stamina, and the path is narrow at times and not always clear. The 2832m pass may be blocked by snow drifts well into the summer. Enquire beforehand at Pont if in doubt.

As well as the easy alternative direct route given to Col del Nivolet via La Croix de l'Arolley detouring the Gran Collet pass, an excellent round trip is Pont-Gran Collet-La Croix de l'Arolley-Pont (some 4h20min in all).

Access: see Walk 17 for Pont.

As far as Col de Nivolet is concerned, in addition to hopes for a summer shuttle bus from Ceresole Reale, the pass is connected to Valle dell'Orco in the south by just one bus (SATTI company, Sundays only, July-August). The bus stop is at the Rif. Savoia car park. The line goes as far as Pont Canavese and its railway station, from where there are connections with Ivrea and Turin.

Note: the narrow 16km Ceresole Reale-Col del Nivolet road to the 2615m pass is generally kept open 15/5-15/10.

Car parking is possible at both the start and end points of the walk.

Stage One: ascent to Gran Collet (2h30min)
From Pont (1960m) walk through the camping ground and follow the path S along the right bank of the torrent up the Vallone di Seyvaz. Some 15min on, opposite a group of huts on the other bank where the access path for Rif. Vittorio Emanuele II turns upwards, a narrow path heads up right, marked by a yellow "2A" on a rock and is easy to miss. The climb is stiff and immediate, but the path is good though narrow. Bearing gradually leftish (SSW) it heads for abandoned Alp. de Seyvaz (2358m, a good 1h this far), the realm of marmots. At the head of the valley is the Grand Etret glacier overshadowed by the Denti del Broglio SSE.

"Gran Collet" painted on a rock indicates the path which continues S a little longer. Waymarking also consists of the occasional 2A in yellow and faded white stripes or arrows. Turning W soon, you climb through a series of grassy basins, many of which will be occupied by ibex females and their inquisitive young who often spy on visitors from giddy outcrops.

Gran Paradiso, view during ascent to Gran Collet

The path climbs steadily and steeply in parts, marked by small cairns. At the last ample terrace preceding the pass, visible now, a photographic stop is called for if you haven't already exhausted the possibilities (note that from the pass itself the view is partially obscured). From ESE to NE is the stunning sweep taking in Ciarforon, Tresenta, the shiny metal roof of Rif. Vittorio Emanuele II beneath Gran Paradiso, then Piccolo Paradiso and Becca di Montandayne, to name but a few.

The final stretch cuts up the right flank of a dirt and snow covered slope to the ample saddle of the Gran Collet (2832m), where a squawking flock of alpine choughs awaits crumbs.

Though not on a par with the preceding valley, interesting new views W and S range over the ample Piano del Nivolet dominated by M. Taou Blanc WNW, and Punta Basei WSW, interspersed with small glacier and snow pockets.

(In descent 1h30min should suffice for this stage.)

Stage Two: descent to Alp. du Gran Collet (40min)
The path heads WNW down a dirt slope and back onto grassy terrain bejewelled with piercing blue gentians, and riddled with

marmot burrow entrances as well as a few lakes. Where the path as such disappears, cairns point the way across the grassy slopes to wind down easily to the Piano del Nivolet, where you join the main path in the vicinity of the ruined huts of Alp. du Gran Collet (2403m). *The name Nivolet comes from an old word for snow.*

(Allow 1h in ascent for this stage).

Alternative direct route from Pont via La Croix de l'Arolley (1h) to Alp. du Gran Collet (40min)

At Pont, behind the Hotel Gran Paradiso with its car park and camping ground, take signposted path n.3. It climbs easily W through larch wood and alpenrose close to a waterfall (right), then the gradient increases dramatically as you zigzag up the steep escarpment to the prominent old wooden cross, La Croix de l'Arolley (2310m, 1h this far).

You cross expanses of rock polished by the slow passage of an ancient glacier, heading SW into the wide Piano del Nivolet, a glacial valley where silt transported by water has accumulated over time and transformed the valley into an important grazing area, as the presence of large herds of sheep and cows testifies. *The sole "negative" note to this pastoral idyll comes from the local shepherds who report the constant risk the lambs run from attacks by golden eagles who evidently single them out as easier prey than marmots. The fertile conditions also mean an abundant and unusual range of flora.*

Keeping to the left side of the open valley, just under 30min on undulating ground should see you in the vicinity of the stone skeleton of the Alp. du Gran Collet buildings (2403m). The path from Gran Collet descends here.

(Some 1h10min for the reverse direction.)

Stage Three: ascent to Col del Nivolet (1h20min)

Ten minutes left (SW) along the flat valley are more old farm buildings, namely Alp. du Nivolet (2399m), where the now wide track climbs briefly. Several bridges lead across the meanders of the torrent amongst densely flowered high altitude meadows, with record concentrations of early flowering white buttercup-like *Ranunculus pyrenaeus* along with white and yellow pasque flowers. Some 30min on, the path joins the surfaced road at the northernmost vehicle limit.

The two large Laghi del Nivolet (2526m) are soon reached, then on the right the first of the two refuges, Rif. Savoia (2532m). *Originally one of the king's hunting lodges, it is more like a hotel nowadays, with souvenirs, tourists and a large car park, and lacks the mountain refuge atmosphere. However an overnight stay includes sheets and a hot shower.* Fifteen minutes up the road past a second lake and off to the left in a panoramic position is quieter Rif. Città di Chivasso (2604m), reserved for walkers and mountaineers. *It was built for military purposes around 1940. The helpful custodian is very knowledgeable on the area's paths and climbs. The only "but" concerns the water - in short supply as it is pumped from a nearby lake, and unsuitable for drinking purposes. The building is lit with soft gas light, however solar panels were being installed at the time of writing. With luck you might catch a glimpse of the ermine which regularly appears hoping for scraps after dinner time.*

The actual pass, Col del Nivolet (2612m), is only a matter of minutes up the road, and together with the marvellous angle onto Punta Basei W from here, a whole new world of stunning mountain ranges - most notably the three Levanna peaks SSE - bordering France and its Vanoise National Park and lakes opens up at your feet.

(Reverse direction: at least 1h.)

RIF. CITTÀ DI CHIVASSO tel:0124/953150. CAI, sleeps 30 (29/6-20/9)
HOTEL FIOR DI ROCCIA (Pont) tel:0165/95478 (20/6-20/9)
RIF. ALBERGO SAVOIA tel:0165/94141. Private, sleeps 40 (20/6-20/9)
TOURIST OFFICE CERESOLE REALE tel:0124/953121-953186
TOURIST OFFICE DEGIOZ tel:0165/905816 (seasonal)

WALKING IN ITALY'S GRAN PARADISO

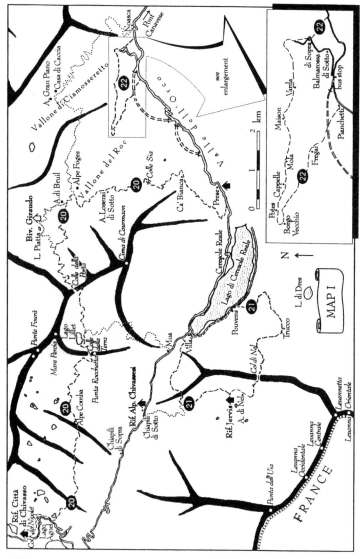

120

> **WALK 20** *(see map I, p.120)*
> ## *Valle dell'Orco -*
> ## *The Royal Game Track Traverse*

via Col del Nivolet - start of path n.550 (30min) - Colle della Terra (2h) - Colle della Porta (1h10min) - Alpe Foges junction (1h40min) - Colle Sia (1h) - Ceresole Reale (1h40min)
Total walking time: **8h (1-2 days suggested)**

A marvellous panoramic route of no more than average difficulty along the most extensive surviving lengths of the original mule-track constructed for the royal hunting parties in the mid-1800s. Sweeping views, adventurous walking in desolate landscapes, featuring very few other humans but plenty of animals. Probably one of the best walks covered in this guide.

Following an initial long, high panoramic coast, the first pass, Colle della Terra, marks an "entry" into more desolate inner valleys below towering peaks. You skirt around Cima di Courmaon and descend upper Vallone del Roc touching on a series of picturesque shepherds' huts, starting at 2250m. All in total abandon now, they constitute sizeable clusters of dry stone work. The last leg drops through wood on the northern flank of the main Valle dell'Orco.

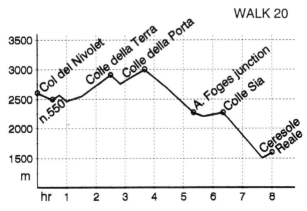

More manageable chunks of the walk are easily bitten off and shorter round walks possible - for instance the route as far as Lago Lillet then descent to Mua, not far from Ceresole Reale.

The walk can also be stretched out over two days and even extended to Noasca, through an overnight stay in Biv. Giraudo (often referred to as Biv. Margherita). It involves a brief detour off the main path, and walkers must be equipped with sleeping and cooking gear, not to mention food. The tiny hut has six bunk beds, some old blankets and the water supply is the nearby lake.

A note of warning: as the complete itinerary is very long, an early start is essential and extra time should be allowed for unclear waymarking, collapsed stretches of path and snow cover, including a gently sloping permanent snow field in the proximity of Colle della Porta, where gaiters can be handy. Not to be underestimated are mist and low cloud, which make orientation decidedly difficult. It is inadvisable to set out on the route in uncertain weather. The helpful custodian at Rif. Città di Chivasso knows the area well, should you require more information before starting out.

The storms in the area are reputedly caused by wind imps letting loose cloud masses at their will from strategic passes, then setting off thunder and lightning with their clashes. The good news is that the whereabouts of Col del Nivolet have long been renowned for the presence of the ephemeral White Dames, white-robed creatures who flit across steep mountainsides and through avalanches to pluck out unfortunate mountaineers.

A note regarding accommodation at Ceresole Reale, the end point: apart from centrally located Albergo Sport and several others strung out down the road, an interesting alternative is the Gran Paradiso Hotel at Prese. Though less opulant nowadays, and moderately priced, this ex Gran Hotel once hosted VIPs such as King Vittorio Emanuele II and his family, as well as the great 19th century Italian poet and statesman Giosuè Carducci, Nobel Prize for Literature, who composed his ode *Piemonte* here.

Access: see Walk 19 for Col del Nivolet.

Ceresole Reale is served by the year-round SATTI bus to the railhead of Pont Canavese (hence connections with Ivrea or Turin).

If you are driving up from Ceresole Reale, stop at the parking area near the eighth hairpin bend after Lago Agnel, and subtract

30min from the walk time. However unless you have access to two vehicles it is a long way to return to pick up your car.

Stage One: descent from Col del Nivolet to start of path n.550 (30min)

As an alternative to the not unpleasant walk down the road from Col del Nivolet, you can take the old game track starting in the vicinity of Rif. Città di Chivasso. It leads SE via a small lake, alias the refuge's water supply, and winds down to the road supported by some interesting built-up stonework. Shortcuts save you the final bends to an unnamed lake at 2461m. In a beautiful position high above the dammed lakes, it looks directly over upper Valle dell'Orco to the crest with Cima del Carro (WSW), Punta dell'Uja (S), then the Levanne pyramids (ESE), interspersed with small ice fields. (45min in the opposite direction.)

Stage Two: traverse via Colle della Terra (2h) to Lago Lillet (20min)

A wooden signpost marks the start of the wide track (n.550) which bears S at first to round Costa della Civetta, then due E, pratically parallel to the valley below. The track, with tidy stone borders, is in good condition on this long panoramic level stretch, and it is easy to imagine the processions of horses bearing privileged hunters and their entourages. The watercourses crossed run down from isolated lakes scattered over a vast ex-glacial area out of sight above, on the southern flanks of the crest linking Punta Violetta and Punte Fourà (so named for a "hole" in its crest, visible from afar).

After a second group of old stone huts (Alpe Comba, 2549m) the track curves leftish to cross a watercourse, then starts its steady climb towards the first pass. *Loose rock and earth prevail, providing meagre yet still attractive pasture for the chamois observable here, along with the ibex.* A wooden signpost marks Colle della Terra (2911m), so called for the "terra" or soil instead of rock here. The wide saddle separates insignificant Punta Rocchetta (S) and the crest that descends from Mare Percia (NE, with its "pierced" peak). The landscape changes dramatically now with high walls sheltering the milky-blue lake, the next destination, while Colle della Porta is ahead E.

The tight zigzags that lead downwards have collapsed in parts but are easily detoured, and Lago Lillet (2765m) in its glacial cirque soon reached. *Surprisingly, the high altitude desolate setting features the hardy orange and purple alpine toadflax and the tiny white blooms of chamois cress.*

Shortly after crossing the lake's outlet, a small cairn and red and white waymarking right indicate the long and steep but useful *alternative access/exit path for Mua.* It drops southwards via a series of abandoned pasture and huts followed by larch forest, to emerge on the Col del Nivolet road at Mua, not far from a camping ground and the northernmost extremity of the Ceresole Reale lake. 2h should suffice in descent, and 3h upwards.

Stage Three: via Colle della Porta (50min) to the 2273m path junction above Alpe Foges (1h40min)

Past the lakeside the path reappears in its wide form, and climbs gradually E with the usual restful curves. Minor peaks La Cuccagna and Cima di Courmaon (SE) separate the path from the main valley now. N.550 follows a moraine ridge left behind by a retreating glacier, and keeps right to avoid the bulk of the permanent snow field, with a final curve back left at the last moment to Colle della Porta (3002m). This "porta" or door opens onto a further wild and ample basin, in the shade of Testa del Gran Etrèt.

Head down the snow-covered slope, without losing sight of the vestiges of the track as it winds down gradually into the immense rubble-filled valley. You are led into the upper Vallone del Roc, below an imposing semicircle of peaks from the Denti del Broglio (aka Cima di Breuil), Becca di Monciair and Ciarforon further around NNE with its pocket glacier. Biv. Giraudo, a small red hut, can be seen ENE.

At about 2700m (some 45min from the pass), as a series of streams is crossed, the path heads decidedly down right in zigzags.

Detour to Biv. Giraudo (30min + 30min)

At this point, providing visibility is good, those intending to break the walk and stay overnight at the hut should go left at two small cairns. It's a matter of making your own way over fallen rocks, as no path as such exists for this stretch. Another stream needs to be crossed, then more clambering and past Lago Piatta to reach Biv.

Ettore and Margherita Giraudo (2630m, 30min). In mist or low cloud it could be tricky locating the hut.

The descent is a little more straightforward, down an old game track SSW into the marshy basin (see below) past Alpe di Bruil (2387m, or Alpe di Broglio) to where cairns and the main track resume (30min).

(From Ceresole Reale the total ascent as far as the hut takes 4h30min.)

From the Biv. Giraudo turn-off, the main route descends for some way to reach a fertile marshy platform high above and overlooking a cluster of stone huts (Alpe Breuillet, aka Alpe Broglietto). The path as such disappears for a while, and only the occasional cairn or red stripe is to be found. Follow the lower edge of the shelf and prepare to ford the icy torrent, with the guarantee of a clearer path on the other side. Cairns reappear immediately as the route from Biv. Giraudo joins up, and soon down right the wide track resumes its way, leading to the marked path junction at 2273m above a ruined group of stone huts, Alpe Foges.

Extension via Alpe Gran Piano (1h30min) to Noasca (2h30min)

This "extension" means completing the original horse-track route (n.550). However it means 4h more from here, and a longer descent as Noasca is 500m lower in terms of altitude than Ceresole Reale.

Left (E) then, n.550 continues on a level high on the northern flank of Vallone del Roc above several groupings of old stone huts. After a brief stretch northwards it enters the Vallone di Ciamosseretto, and crosses the stream beneath Alpe Gran Piano (2379m).

The descent finally starts SE, via the old stone hunting lodge Casa di Caccia (2222m), now Park property. Glacier-smoothed rocks follow, then there are never-ending bends cutting the pasture slopes beneath M. Castello. At 1650m you are joined by the path from Biv. Ivrea in Vallone di Noaschetta. Via more old shepherds' huts such as Sassa (1353m), still occasionally used in the summer, then finally into the wood. It emerges at the small township of Noasca (1061m) on the main road, squeezed in between immense cliffs on the floor of Valle dell'Orco. *As well as a small hotel, youth hostel and food shops, there is a National Park Visitors' Centre here.*

(In the reverse direction, allow 3h30min in ascent as far as A. Gran Piano then 1h30min to the 2273m junction.)

Stage Four: descent via Colle Sia (1h) to Ceresole Reale (1h40min)
At the 2273m junction, take the right branch (n.542 now) to a nearby spread of "roches moutonnées". These aligned glacially-modelled boulders close off the mouth of a pretty marshy basin soft with cotton grass, and housing the old Alpe Breuillet huts at the far end.

Numerous ibex and chamois occupy the pastures, with the addition of the odd herd of cows. The path heads S now. Red paint marks the wide track, mostly on a level. A sizeable settlement comprising a variety of picturesque stone houses, Alpe Loserai di Sotto (2210m) is passed some 20min along. They are worth a second look for their intricate construction techniques.

The track climbs a little in wide curves to Colle Sia (2274m), a depression well below Cima di Courmaon that leads from the Vallone del Roc into the Valle dell'Orco.

The descent starts in earnest and drops S down a bare hillside to more old stone buildings. The path peters out in several points but red/white waymarking guides you. At the second sizeable group of ruins (2002m) a large cairn marks the point where the GTA route merges. (A further if longer exit at this point consists in following the GTA left NE, to join the old houses referred to in Walk 22.)

Keep right down through larch, alpenrose and bilberries, to scenically sited Ca' Bianca (1942m) in a clearing.

From here the path heads decisively SW into a tall conifer wood, where woodpeckers and chamois are not uncommon. Glimpses of the Ceresole Reale dam wall are frequent, but it never seems to get any closer. Laden raspberry thickets and laburnum announce the proximity of a dirt road and a Park signpost. Briefly down right is the asphalted main road, not far from a bus stop, near Prese. However the centre of Ceresole Reale with shops, Tourist Office and Park Visitors' Centre, is some 20min (2km) uphill near the lakeside.

(3h30min in ascent should suffice for this stage.)

The village probably owes its name to "cherries", whereas "Reale" (royal) was added in 1862 by King Vittorio Emanuele II, in exchange for concession of hunting rights for chamois and ibex. It is a peaceful place, with no tales of devils or evil doings, only fairies who leave gifts hanging in trees.

RIF. CITTÀ DI CHIVASSO (Col del Nivolet) tel:0124/953150. CAI, sleeps 30 (30/6-20/9)

RIF. ALBERGO SAVOIA (Col del Nivolet) tel:0165/94141. Private, sleeps 40 (20/6-20/9)

BIV. E. & M. GIRAUDO, CAI, sleeps 6 (always open)

LAGO SERRÙ (on the Col del Nivolet road): several bar/restaurants in the vicinity offer lodgings midsummer.

ALBERGO GRAN PARADISO (Prese, Ceresole Reale) tel:0124/953116 (20/6-10/9)

ALBERGO SPORT (Ceresole Reale) tel:0124/953187 (open year-round)

GRAN PARADISO HOTEL (Noasca) tel:0124/901118

OSTELLO - YOUTH HOSTEL (Noasca) tel:0124/901107 8.30-9.30am/3.30-8.30pm (open year-round). Sleeps 56. Membership I.Y.H. necessary - can join on the spot, no age limit. Meals available.

POSTO TAPPA GTA (Fonti Minerali, Ceresole Reale) C/O tel:0124/953117 (1/6-30/9)

TOURIST OFFICE CERESOLE REALE tel:0124/953186-953121 (seasonal)

TOURIST OFFICE NOASCA tel:0124/901001-901005 (seasonal)

WALK 21 *(see map I, p.120)*

Valle dell'Orco - Beneath the Tre Levanne

---

via Villa - Rif. Jervis (2h) - Col di Nel (1h15min) - Pouvens (1h45min) - Villa (20min)
Total walking time: **5h20min (1 day suggested)**

This itinerary is dominated by the three majestic Levanne peaks, as in fact is the entire lower valley between Col del Nivolet and Ceresole Reale. The pyramidal line-up, averaging 3500m, forms a stretch of the Italian-French border.

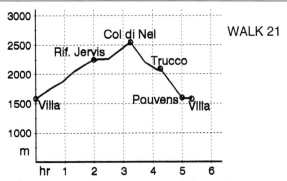

The walk as far as Rif. Jervis is easy and the ample panoramic flats and immense glacially smoothed rock slabs in the vicinity of the refuge are perfect for picnics. The extension via Col di Nel is less frequented, apart from the chamois and marmots, and while steep in parts, is relatively trouble-free. Snow cover on this stretch may persist into July.

Access: see Walk 20.

Those with a car can park at Villa, the starting point. It is some 2.5km after Ceresole Reale, at the end of the lake. On foot allow 25min.

Stage One: ascent from Villa to Rif. Jervis (2h)

From the small chapel on the road at Villa (1583m), signposting for Rif. Jervis (n.530) points W and over the torrent. It climbs NW through a fresh larch wood alive with song birds. The path is clear with the occasional red paint splashes. Thirty minutes on is the first of several stone buildings (A. Foeira, 1753m) next to a stream which is crisscrossed several times. A second group of huts, A. Bagnetti (1877m), occupies a picturesque marshy area dotted with fluffy cotton grass and bordered by rowan trees. Larch and pink alpenrose shrubs then accompany you to a lookout point (approx. 2000m) where views take in Punta di Galisia and Punta Basei (WNW), the modest ridge N, as well as providing a glimpse of the Levanne and glacier S.

Descending towards Levionaz d'en Bas, with the Herbetet in the background (Walk 12)

Rif. Vittorio Emanuele II - Walk 17

Sea of white ranunculus, Piano del Nivolet, with Punta Basei - Walk 19

Further on, near yet another abandoned hut (A. Degranè, 2049m), the path from Chiapili di Sotto (see Alternative access) joins up and you head S now out of the trees. The refuge soon comes into sight. High left above cascading Rio di Nel in its narrow gorge, the path winds through shrubs and bears right over glacially smoothed rock and across a bridge.

Rif. Jervis (2250m) *is a model alpine refuge with helpful staff, and was named after Guglielmo Iervis, a WW2 partisan and mountaineer from Ivrea, the town at the easternmost end of Valle d'Aosta and home to the CAI branch that owns the refuge. Its position is enthusing, in front of the three Levanne peaks which shelter the Ghiacciaio di Nel and old abandoned moraine ridges. Furthermore it stands on the very edge of the Piano di Nel, an ample basin excavated by an extensive glacier and successively occupied by a lake, now silted up. The small pumping station nearby is connected with the pipeline from Lago Serrù to the Villa hydroelectric power station.* (Allow 1h10min in descent.)

Alternative access from Chiapili di Sotto (1h30min)

Though on the road, the spacious refuge-cum-hostel Rif. Alpinisti Chivassesi, alias Rif. G. Muzio (1667m), is a convenient place to stay. Not far away, on the opposite side of the road, path n.531 heads S through wood to climb on the left-hand bank of Rio di Nel via A. Glassetti (1815m) to join the path from Villa to Rif. Jervis.

Stage Two: ascent to Col di Nel (1h15min)

Return to the bridge and proceed right past the pumping station. A faintly marked route skirts the easternmost edge of the ex-lake. Head for the stone buildings of A. di Nel (2264m), but watch out for marshy zones. Red waymarking reappears along the left-hand side of the stream. As you enter the final cirque beneath the glacier, about 30min from the refuge, red painted letters on a large rock slab announce Col di Nel, confirmed by a prominent cairn - turn up sharp left. E for the most part, the faint but well marked path climbs steadily and steeply at times, through brightly flowered mixed rock-earth terrain, with some snow cover to be expected early summer. Chamois are a common sight.

The pass, Col di Nel (2551m), occupies an excellent position for appreciating the magnificent head of the valley, with the remnants of Ghiacciaio di Nel and the Levanne peaks, not to mention the vast views E and onto the Ceresole Reale lake. *Silver-bearing lead, commonly found in Valle dell'Orco, was once mined in the vicinity of the pass, by Christians as legend would have it.* (40min should suffice in the opposite direction.)

Stage Three: descent via Trucco (1h) to Pouvens (45min), hence Villa (20min)

The clear descent path drops (E) quickly down grassy slopes via a series of small platforms, plenty of helpful cairns showing the way. After a stretch alongside an old extensive rockslip (left), you reach a low hut ruin and a boggy lake. Down right beneath the modest peak la Trucci, a larger lake follows (approx. 2250m, not shown on maps). The path soon bears right (S) and drops into a vast pasture basin, views ranging E taking in Lago di Dres (SE). The flora is brighter and thicker now, notably gentians and yellow avens. You drop onto another flowered platform, its marshy terrain perfect for the tiny purplish-white flowers of insect-devourer common butterwort. Keeping S, traverse well below a ruined hut (A. Manda, 2210m), and down to what must have been a sizeable farming settlement once (A. Pian Mutta, 2130m). Make your way among the ruins, and keep right (S) via the occasional cairn and over to a shallow earth gully.

You climb out of it among alpenrose to join the access path for Biv. Leonesi, whose grey roof is visible with the aid of binoculars up SW in a northern snow-filled gully beneath the Levanne. Turn down left guided by clear red paint markings along the grassy ridge to an old stone hut, referred to as Trucco (2098m) on maps.

You need the path that drops left, NE for the most part, into tall conifer wood, punctuated by numerous oversized red ant nests. After a loop via an old farm, it continues left (NW) to cross a stream, before emerging at Pouvens (1598m), a group of houses on the lakeside. (In ascent from here allow a good 3h.)

Left around the narrow road will lead you past the Villa power station and back to Villa, the starting point.

At the time of writing plans were under way for a "pedestrians only" route around the lake via the dam wall, which is currently out of bounds to the public. This will make an alternative return to

Ceresole Reale possible by heading right (E) at Pouvens along the lake's southernmost shore.

RIF. CASA ALPINISTI CHIVASSESI/RIF. G. MUZIO tel:0124/ 953141. CAI, sleeps 35 (15/6-15/9 + weekends and public hols 15/ 3-15/11)
RIF. JERVIS tel:0124/953140. CAI, sleeps 23 (1/7-31/8 + weekends June & Sept)
TOURIST OFFICE CERESOLE REALE tel:0124/953186-953121 (seasonal)

WALK 22 *(see map I, p.120)*
Valle dell'Orco - Old Frescoed Villages

---

via main road above Noasca - Maison (1h10min) - Potes (30min) - Pianchetti (1h) - main road starting point (20min)
Total walking time: **3h (1 day suggested)**

An intriguing round trip on an old paved path that threads its way through some unique alpine villages, dating back to at least the 1700s and only recently abandoned. Wandering through the peaceful overgrown settlements disturbed only by the odd barking dog belonging to the reticent shepherds who make their summer residence here, modern-day visitors can get a feeling of medium-altitude (1500m) mountain life. Strictly local materials, namely stone and some timber, were used to craft houses and huts built around huge fallen boulders, available space and "free" walls exploited to the utmost. Apart from communal buildings such as a church, school and oven for the traditional rye bread, there are fascinating colourful religious frescoes and numerous family votive shrines along the way. A special mention is due for the ingenious "crutin", low stone-roofed huts used for dairy storage - villagers would divert watercourses through the huts to keep the products cool. While in the Valle dell'Orco don't neglect to purchase some delicious "toma", the local cheese that used to be made in villages

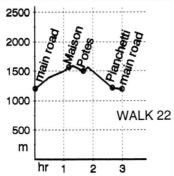

WALK 22

such as these.

A whole day could be spent exploring the string of hamlets and wandering along the paths, the only connection with the valley, apart from the rare later addition of one or two mechanised cableways. After a brief climb (300m) to the first village, the route is on a level with a final descent down the lower part of Vallone del Roc, and back to the main road near the starting point. No difficulty is involved. Any time between April and November is suitable.

In an attempt to safeguard the precious cultural heritage of these hamlets, the National Park has designated the route one of its "Sentiero Natura", including the occasional "reflection point" for guided walks, and marked pole pointers, which cows grazing on the open hillsides tend to knock over.

For any further information contact the Park Visitors' Centre at Noasca tel:0124/90070.

Access: Noasca is on the year-round (SATTI company) bus service from Pont Canavese. Some 1.5km above Noasca is the start of the "Sentiero Natura". Either ask the driver to drop you off here, mentioning the old villages by name, or get off a little further along at the bus stop for Balmarossa, just before the long road tunnel leading to Ceresole Reale.

Drivers can park on the main road at the start of the "Sentiero Natura" where the road widens, immediately following the series of hairpin bends above Noasca.

Stage One: via Varda (1h) and Maison (10min) to Potes (30min)
At approx. 1195m on the roadside look for the National Park wooden post for the "Sentiero Natura" together with the distinctive GTA (Grande Traversata delle Alpi) red and white markings. The path winds upwards through hazel trees to old terracing, now inhabited by bright green lizards and butterflies. A narrow asphalt

road is crossed and you traverse the hamlet of Balmarossa di Sopra (1275m). After re-crossing the road, the old paved path soon appears and climbs high on the left bank of Torrente Ciamosseretto, the cause of noticeable damage downstream at Noasca late 1993. A couple more encounters with the road and at just over 30min you reach a small parking area (approx. 1400m). (Ignore the path which heads right to cross the cascading torrent on the way to the Vallone di Ciamosseretto - another worthwhile excursion). Keep straight on up the path, wider and in better condition now, to wind up through a rich mixed wood including wild cherry, sycamore and chestnut. Dry stone walls border long stretches of paved path, and occasional shrines have been fitted into niches.

At 1h is the first village, Varda (1500m), worth an exploratory detour off the main path. Some 10min further on around the hillside, after a stream crossing, is Maison or Meison, the Italianised version (1567m). *This is the largest village and has some fascinating constructions. A visit to the diminutive whitewashed church decorated with paintings of saints is recommended (first turning down left). Then on the far edge of the village is the school complete with old wooden benches, chilly outside toilet, and teacher's lodgings upstairs. It was in use until the mid-1960s.*

A brief climb leads to a marvellous panoramic stretch on a cliff edge with giddy views to the Valle Orco road and underlying hamlets. Ahead (W) is the Cima di Courmaon.

Mola (1591m), the highest of this line of hamlets is next with its communal oven and frescoes, followed shortly by Cappelle (1585m) which features a fountain (drinking water) and barking dogs. A brief descent through tall grass takes you to the torrent and the cluster of huts that comprise Potes (1500m), below a lovely waterfall. (Some 1h30min in the opposite direction).

Stage Two: descent via Fregai (30min) to Pianchetti (30min) and starting point on main road (20min)

After the bridge crossing, the path climbs onto a rocky spur below a chapel and the hamlet of Borgo Vecchio (1567m). At this point the red and white-marked GTA climbs away to the right whereas the Sentiero Natura starts its descent down the valley (arrow marking). Flowered pastures are crossed (no apparent waymarking) followed by a further brief climb. Once you're past a side watercourse in light wood, the path reappears in paved form intent on serious descent at last. Zigzags lead to the tightly-knit houses of Fregai (1428m).

Soon you drop unexpectedly into a delicious beech wood, which lasts almost all the rest of the way down to the settlement of Pianchetti (1220m). Thread your way through the old and new houses, complete with frescoes and inhabitants, down to the road.

Turn left here and proceed to where the main road from Ceresole Reale emerges from the tunnel, in the vicinity of a bus stop. To return to the starting point, continue a further 20min E along the road. (Just under 2h reverse timing.)

GRAN PARADISO HOTEL (Noasca) tel:0124/901118
OSTELLO - YOUTH HOSTEL (Noasca) tel:0124/901107 8.30-9.30am/3.30-8.30pm (open year-round). Sleeps 56. Membership I.Y.H. necessary - can join on the spot, no age limit. Meals available.
TOURIST OFFICE NOASCA tel:0124/901001-901005 (seasonal)

WALK 23 *(see map J, p.135)*

Vallone di Piantonetto - Beyond the Dam

---

via San Giacomo - Lago di Teleccio (2h) - Rif. Pontese (1h) - Muanda di Teleccio (30min return time) - Lago di Teleccio (40min) - San Giacomo (1h30min)
Total walking time: **5h40min (1 day suggested)**

The inclusion of an itinerary in a valley whose upper reaches have been dammed for hydroelectricity purposes may seem incongruous. With its towering gneiss flanks, long desolate Vallone di Piantonetto is a curious anomaly. Above the dam a beautiful ample grazing basin is revealed at 2200m, surrounded by a series of vast rock shelves, precursors to a chain of imposing peaks, the 3650m likes of Roccia Viva and Torre del Gran San Pietro. Sheltering in cirques are two surviving glacier pockets, which feed both the pasture and the dam. A refuge stands on the edge of the basin, a testimony to the

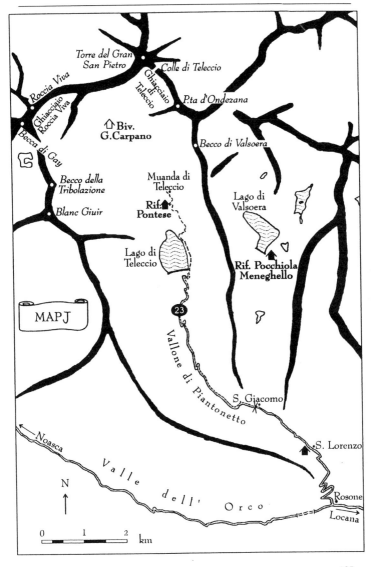

growing popularity of the valley with walkers and rock climbers.

As far as the 23 million cu.m dam Lago di Teleccio goes, construction on the site of a pre-existing silted-up glacial lake at 1917m dates back to 1955. In combination with flows from the similarly dammed lakes of Ceresole Reale, Valsoera and Eugio, it supplies the historic power plant at Rosone.

The extensive hydroelectric system in this southern sector of the Park is supervised by the Turin-based electricity board AEM (Azienda Energetica Municipale) which started operations in the Valle dell'Orco back in the 1920s.

16.5km W of the township of Pont Canavese, Vallone di Piantonetto breaks away from main Valle dell'Orco near Rosone (715m). After an initial stretch of tight curves as it climbs through a chestnut wood, the narrow surfaced road enters the actual valley and crosses to the right-hand side of the torrent near the main village of San Lorenzo (4km, 1045m), then continues NW to the tiny hamlet of San Giacomo (4km). Here the asphalt ends, and a faded sign forbids unauthorised vehicles to proceed. The 6km of dirt road from here on are both the work and property of the AEM whose staff carry out regular maintenance, as well as using it daily - meaning you can expect to meet heavy-duty machinery on the road occasionally. However, as a visit on a summer Sunday will prove, visiting motorists - tourists, walkers and mountaineers alike - ignore the sign and drive all the way up to the dam.

The immediate dam area is occupied by a conglomeration of run-down buildings, very few of which are in use nowadays. In a late 1992 agreement with the National Park, the AEM undertook the task of cleaning up the surroundings and dismantling unused structures. However several are to be left to house experimentation on solar energy, beginning in the near future and funded partly by the European Union. The only undecided issue at present concerns the enforcement or otherwise of the road block after San Giacomo.

The walk itself begins at San Giacomo, but continues well beyond the dam and is entirely problem-free.

Though not described here, a further recommended excursion is to Rif. Pocchiola-Meneghello (2440m) at Lago Valsoera. The signed path for the long 1315m climb starts out at San Giacomo and demands some 4h30min in ascent.

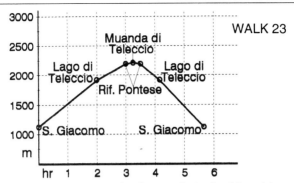

Access: see above description for drivers. Quite frankly, without a car it is hardly worth walking the 14km up the road from Rosone, where you find the nearest bus stop on the year-round Pont Canavese-Ceresole Reale SATTI run.

Stage One: from San Giacomo to Lago di Teleccio (2h)

The hamlet of San Giacomo (1125m) has but two permanent inhabitants, in addition to an ageless wiry goatherd. It also boasts a tiny church, site of festivities held every July.

Park here and follow the narrowing road, soon unsurfaced, over to the left-hand side of the valley, and up through several small-size seasonal dairy settlements. A couple of intriguing instances of traditional constructions built against boulders are passed. *The lightly wooded zones feature bright orange lilies alongside the wine-coloured martagon variety.* Via a series of hairpins and a narrow stretch cut into the rock wall, you cross the valley well beneath the 515m long, 80m high dam wall. There follows a short rock tunnel and the first of the maintenance buildings, not to mention the start of the 2km underground passage which carries a gigantic conduit and staff members beneath the mountains E to connect with the dam of Lago di Valsoera.

Up at the dam wall of Lago di Teleccio (1917m), Rif. Pontese is visible NNW in its commanding position, a dark building with yellow shutters. However well beyond it literally tower Torre del Gran San Pietro (NNW), with massive Becco di Valsoera N.

Shelter in Vallone di Piantonetto

Stage Two: ascent to Rif. Pontese (1h)

The wide track keeps to the eastern side of the lake, leaving the jumble of derelict structures behind. Some 1km along it becomes a path and winds up the steep rock flank before bearing left over a rock spur. Past a junction (for difficult path n.560 to Rif. Pocchiola-Meneghello) then NW over a series of glacially smoothed rocks and grass to the vast slab where Rif. Pontese (2200m) now stands. *The original Piantonetto hut, built in 1889 at the time the surrounding peaks were being discovered by the pioneer alpinists, stood much further up the valley.*

The amphitheatre, starting from W and moving clockwise, is encompassed by Blanc Giuir, Becco della Tribolazione, Becca di Gay, Roccia Viva, Torre del Gran San Pietro, Punta d'Ondezana and Becco di Valsoera, which average out at 3500m.

Stage Three: extension to Muanda di Teleccio (30min return time)

Mandatory path n.558 proceeds essentially NW keeping to the right-hand bank of the main torrent. You stroll into the glacial cirque alias vast pasture basin watered by streams fed from the higher glaciers - Ghiacciaio di Teleccio, due N behind a rock barrier, and Ghiacciaio Roccia Viva, NW. *The marshy terrain sports specialised flora such as the insectivorous common butterwort with its small purplish-white blooms, and the solitary whitish flowers of Grass-of-Parnassus.*

Some 15min along in a central position are the old huts known as Muanda di Teleccio (2217m), the term "muanda" denoting a high altitude summer farm. *Reference to another farm in the area, the Muanda d'Ondezana, has surfaced from medieval records as the inhabitants of Cogne were granted pasture rights there in 1206 by the Bishop of Aosta. Payment took the form of 30 cheeses to be delivered on St. Martin's Day, November 11th. To reach the site from the south, however, the shepherds were obliged to undertake the lengthy traverse of 3326m Colle di Teleccio. Today in place of the livestock are large numbers of chamois, shy creatures who make for the surrounding slopes if disturbed.*

(Visible in good conditions on a further rock shelf NW is Biv. Carpano. At 2865m it is a destination for experienced walkers only as the faintly marked path has both steep and exposed stretches, aided in parts. Ibex frequent the area. Allow a good 2h45min in ascent.)

Stage Four: return via Lago di Teleccio (40min) then San Giacomo (1h30min)

As per ascent route.

BIV. CARPANO, CAI, sleeps 4 (always open)
RIF. POCCHIOLA-MENEGHELLO c/o tel:011/5817584. CAI, sleeps 14 (always open, but staffed with meals provided 28/7-27/8). Essentially a bivouac hut, in a converted AEM building
RIF. PONTESE tel: c/o 0124/85905. (Leave message on answering machine. Calls will be answered directly Fri 9-10pm.) Local Alpine Club, sleeps 40 (15/7-27/8 + weekends from May to mid-September)
POSTO TAPPA GTA c/o TRATTORIA DEGLI AMICI (San Lorenzo) tel:0124/800195. Sleeps 12 (open year-round)
TOURIST OFFICE CERESOLE REALE tel:0124/953186-953121 (seasonal)

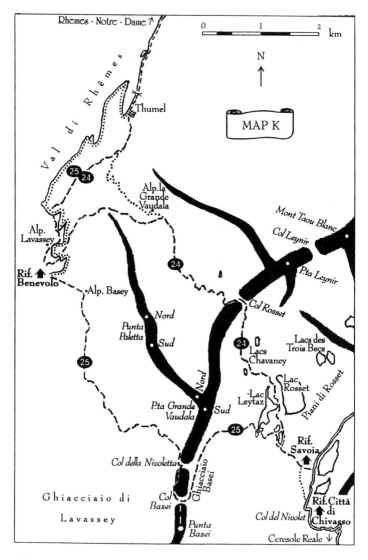

WALK 24 *(see map K, opposite)*
Col del Nivolet/Val di Rhêmes - Col Rosset

via Col del Nivolet - Col Rosset (2h) - Rif. Benevolo (2h) - Thumel (1h10min) - Bruil (50min)
Total walking time: **6h (1-2 days suggested)**

A short stroll above the Col del Nivolet road is the Piani di Rosset plateau consisting of an absolutely beautiful expanse of lakes amidst breathtaking scenery: from the Tre Levanne SSE to the Ciarforon-Gran Paradiso line-up E, without forgetting M. Taou Blanc and massive Punta Basei close by. A full day could easily be spent just wandering and exploring the area, within easy reach of the road and refuges below. (See Walk 19 for more information about Col del Nivolet.)

The walk meanders across this marvellous altopiano to climb to easy 3000m Col Rosset, an ice-free age-old passage to neighbouring Val di Rhêmes. The ensuing descent is the sole section likely to involve any difficulty - a steep detritus-covered flank, a little unstable especially with soft, late-lying snow. Apart from this, the walk is straightforward and suitable for average walkers.

An overnight stop at Rif. Benevolo is unfailingly a pleasant experience, and furthermore makes it feasible to slot into Walk 25 or 28. An added attraction of upper Val di Rhêmes is the unusual and

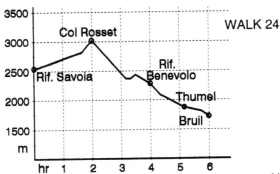

Rif. Città di Chivasso at Col del Nivolet

spectacular Granta Parei peak, briefly SW of the refuge.

Note: Rhêmes-Notre-Dame is used to refer to the grouping of villages in upper Val di Rhêmes, whereas Bruil is the principal settlement.

Access: see Walk 19 for Col del Nivolet.

The end point Bruil (Rhêmes-Notre-Dame) is connected with Aosta by SAVDA company bus all year round, though runs are few and far between. Car parking is possible at both Thumel and Bruil.

Stage One: via Piani di Rosset to Col Rosset (2h)

The walk starts at Rif. Savoia (2532m) - some 15min N down the road from the Col del Nivolet pass and Rif. Città di Chivasso. Ignore popular path 9/A for Col Leynir and look for the Alta Via 4 triangle waymarking for the track to the left of the refuge annex. It leads up E and onto the vast pasture plateau, Piani di Rosset with its lakes. Climbing gently NNW you coast between the two major lakes, Lago Rosset and Lago Leytaz. The outlook is inspiring to say the least.

A good 30min will see you at the far end of the lakes where a steady but short climb begins amongst surprising thick clumps of edelweiss. A wide shiny corridor of mica-schists is next. *The characteristic flora includes brilliant King of the Alps forget-me-not, and a yellow variety of mustard flower similar to a dwarf wallflower. Snow lies in depressions around the path for extended periods, and chamois seem to enjoy lazing in it.* Several more small lakes (Lacs Chanavey) lie along the way to the base of the escarpment where the final 150m (a good 20min) are a series of tight and exacting zigzags to the pass. Multicoloured rock bands are crossed of dark grey-brown, greenstone and pink-tinged limestone.

Col Rosset (3023m) is quite something, with generous views in all directions. However an improvement is possible via the clear path up right (NE) to the trig point: looking back the way you've come, even though the Gran Paradiso is out of sight, ESE is Tresenta then Ciarforon and co., as well as the Col del Nivolet pass with its magnificent backdrop. On the other side Val di Rhêmes features lower but distinct light-coloured Granta Parei WSW and the crest with Punta Tsantelèynaz SW, plus underlying glaciers and continuous moraines. (This path leads on to the 3235m summit of Punta Leynir, meaning "black lake" - for experts only.)

(Allow 1h30min in descent for this stage.)

Stage Two: descent via Alp. la Grande Vaudala (1h10min) to Rif. Benevolo (50min)

On this initial stretch the path literally disappears beneath your boots down the steep scree-earth mix slope. Guided by Alta Via 4 and occasional yellow markings, you embark on a wide curve left, a little exposed, then zigzag right. In all 20min are involved, then the going becomes a little easier on the knees as you return to stable grassed terrain. Amidst flowers and marmots the path keeps to the right-hand side of the valley and torrent, and heads for the old farm buildings visible, Alp. la Grande Vaudala (2338m). However before reaching them, after a side stream crossing, a narrow path (yellow arrows) branches off left to the main torrent where two sturdy timber beams act as a bridge.

Alternative exit to Thumel (1h30min)

This handy exit takes you directly to the floor of the Val di Rhêmes. A little further on from the Rif. Benevolo turn-off are the abandoned farm buildings of Alp. la Grande Vaudala (2338m). Soon the marked path leaves the valley and continues NW down the steep flank to cross the torrent Dora di Rhêmes, terminating at the farm settlement of Thumel (1879m). Shortly downhill is the start of car access and parking area. From here it's 4 asphalted km to Bruil (just under 1h), as per Stage Three.

(In ascent from Thumel, 4h all the way to Col Rosset.)

Near the torrent crossing "R. Benevolo 40min" is painted on a rock, however it usually requires a little longer. The path climbs diagonally (W) across mixed rock flows. *The dry hillside is alive with grasshoppers, whereas the scree is thick with the large plants of the dull pink-violet felted adenostyle flowers.* Continuing on the rather exposed hillside you climb to a shoulder at 2440m (20min from the torrent) and are rewarded by the wonderful spectacle of light-coloured peaks and ice that crown the head of the Val di Rhêmes, in addition to the almost aerial view of the valley floor N.

Over rolling pasture land and hillocks now, guided by propped-up stones and small cairns, you proceed SW to the refuge, visible ahead on an outcrop. You'll probably lose sight of the path as the cattle, which belong to nearby Alp. Lavassey, usually manage to obliterate it, but waymarking is frequently renewed. If you don't manage to come out on the 4WD track just below the refuge, wander over the hillside until a convenient stock descent route presents itself.

Rif. Benevolo (2285m), named after an entomologist from Turin, is a hospitable old-style if smallish refuge, run by qualified guides who know the area like the back of their hand. (They also open mid-March to the end of May for ski tourers.) The catering is great, and breakfast may even include muesli. A regular diner is the sleek fox who drops in after dark for scraps. The tap water is theoretically unsuitable for drinking purposes as it comes from a nearby spring.

(About 3h in ascent from Rif. Benevolo to Col Rosset.)

With time to spare, take the easy path leading to the beautiful upper valley to the source of the Dora di Rhêmes torrent beneath several glaciers.

Stage Three: descent to Thumel (1h10min) and Bruil (50min)
(See also Walk 28 for further details on this section.)

When the time comes to point your boots valleywards, the winding jeep track and cut down the path via a brief aided stretch behind the refuge building. After touching on the track several times, you actually join it at a bridge over the Dora di Rhêmes torrent, and stick with it briefly around left, to a showering cascade. A marked path soon branches off to the right, and leads through delightful landscape with shrubs and plenty of flowers on the banks of the torrent. Several cascades are passed, and just over 1h will see you at the settlement of Thumel (1879m), where you meet the vehicle track. Shortly downhill is the car parking area.

The final stretch means 4km of not unpleasant asphalt through Pelaud (1811m), a picturesque hamlet with a roomy characteristic building converted into a modest hotel. The final destination is the village of Bruil, Rhêmes-Notre-Dame, with its bus stop, hotels and shops.

RIF. BENEVOLO tel:0165/906143. CAI, sleeps 62 (June weekends, 1/7-20/9)
RIF. CITTÀ DI CHIVASSO tel:0124/953150. CAI, sleeps 30 (end June-20/9)
RIF. ALBERGO SAVOIA tel:0165/94141. Private, sleeps 40 (20/6-20/9)
PELAUD guesthouse (Pelaud, Rhêmes-Notre-Dame) tel:0165/936110 (1/6-30/9)
TOURIST OFFICE BRUIL (Rhêmes-Notre-Dame) tel:0165/96114 (seasonal)
TOURIST OFFICE CERESOLE REALE tel:0124/953121-953186

WALK 25 *(see map K, p.140)*

Val di Rhêmes/Col del Nivolet - Punta Basei

---

via Bruil - Thumel (1h) - Rif. Benevolo (1h30min) - Col della Nivoletta (2h30min) - Col Basei (30min) - Punta Basei (1h return time) - Rif. Savoia (Col del Nivolet) (1h30min)
Total walking time: **8h (1-2 days suggested)**

This is a further traverse connecting the Col del Nivolet area with upper Val di Rhêmes. Unlike the other two more straightforward walks 24 & 26, this one involves a glacier crossing, though in essence it means a pleasantly sloping snow field which is crevasse-free. Gaiters could be useful. Furthermore the optional but rewarding ascent to the magnificent viewpoint and 3338m summit Punta Basei has been included, although a sure foot along with experience on ice are the usually quoted requisites. The peak is a popular and closer destination from the Col del Nivolet side.

The area around the incredibly panoramic 3100m cols - both of which are worthwhile return day trips from their respective sides - is somewhat exposed to the elements and the loose terrain requires extra attention. Snow and possibly ice are to be reckoned with at the start and end of the season. August-early September is probably the best period for this itinerary.

Note: there is often confusion between the road pass Col del Nivolet (2612m) and walkers-only Col della Nivoletta (3130m). Different maps use different spellings, but the main distinguishing feature is Nivolet vs. Nivoletta.

Access: see Walk 24 for Bruil, and Walk 19 for Col del Nivolet.

Stage One: access via Thumel (1h) then Rif. Benevolo (1h30min)
From the end of the bus line at the village of Bruil (1723m) take the asphalt road S up to the parking area just before the farming settlement of Thumel (1879m).

A wide signposted path leads alongside the torrent via several cascades and climbs to hospitable Rif. Benevolo (2285m). See Walk

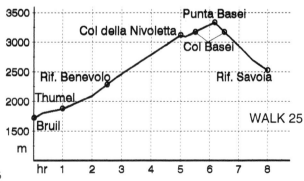

Upper Val di Rhêmes during the ascent to Col della Nivoletta

28, Stage One for more details.

(Allow 2h in the opposite direction.)

Stage Two: ascent to Col della Nivoletta (2h30min)

Near the refuge is yellow painted waymarking on a rock for "Col Nivoletta, Plan des Dames" indicating a path that begins climbing leftish (SE). Five minutes up is a fascinating example of the long livestock stalls built/excavated into the natural slope of the land so as to reduce damage in case of avalanches. The path forks up left once more (whereas another path follows the valley floor). Shortly an old stone-lined V-shaped water channel is crossed and you climb to another long abandoned building (Alpage Basey, 2412m, 20min from the start). From here head right (S) along a dry stone wall. The path regularly disappears and the way is often unclear, so don't proceed too far without seeing a yellow stripe or cairn.

As you climb steadily SSE beneath Punta Paletta, views around the beautiful head of Val di Rhêmes improve with every step - magnificent light limestone Granta Parei (W), then pyramidal Punta Tsantelèynaz WSW, and the series of smaller graceful peaks including Roc du Fond and Roc Basagne above the diminishing glaciers.

The path improves. You may surprise chamois at pasture in a flowered side valley about halfway up. There are several stream traverses followed by permanent expanses of snow, not steep for the most part. Direct your steps towards the frequent yellow waymarking on the rocks ahead. *Beneath Punta Grande Vaudala now, the terrain is shiny, slatey-looking schists and vegetation includes the tough yellowish felted genepi flowers, used by the locals for flavouring spirit.*

Constant but straightforward climbing SSE leads via a rocky outcrop, given as 3061m on maps, where waymarking tends to be a trifle patchy. A final level leg eventually brings you out at the cairn on airy Col della Nivoletta (3130m). The breathtaking crest offers views of Gran Paradiso (ENE), Ciarforon (E), the Levanne line-up (SE), then the lakes nestling in the numerous depressions around Col del Nivolet, where the road is visible.

(1h30min in total for the opposite direction.)

Stage Three: traverse to Col Basei (30min)
To reach southernmost Col Basei at least two alternatives present themselves. The first follows the loose debris crest in brief ascent at first. Special care is needed as there are uncertain and exposed stretches. Alternatively follow the crest briefly then take the faint path cutting down the slope right, avoiding the ascent. You drop into a sort of wide gully and may be joined by walkers on another route from Rif. Benevolo (via Ghiacciaio di Lavassey). Make your own way up left scrambling over fallen rocks to the wide crest from where Col Basei (3176m) is shortly attained.

Punta Basei, straight up the crest S, looks a little like a square castle.

Stage Four: ascent to Punta Basei (1h return time)
The ascent from Col Basei to the summit is reserved for walkers with some climbing experience as the final leg usually involves ice and rock passages and consequently the appropriate equipment (ice pick and crampons). From the col the rounded crest is followed up S to where a top section of Ghiacciaio Basei is encountered and crossed. After a rock climb aided by fixed cable, it's not far to the

metal cross on the spectacular 3338m summit of Punta Basei.

Return carefully the same way.

Stage Five: descent via Piani di Rosset to Rif. Savoia (Col del Nivolet) (1h30min)

The way down traverses a long section of the Ghiacciaio di Basei, but by midsummer the snow cover is usually ice-free so you simply take the well-trodden diagonal piste virtually due N in gradual descent. Some 20min later when you leave the glacier and reach loose rubble-earth terrain, the occasional cairn guides you in a curve around NE and onto a clearer path. Faint red waymarking also becomes apparent.

A rock spur is reached with a bird's-eye view over the Piani di Rosset lakes. Tight zigzags drop down a steep edelweiss-studded flank to the southern end of Lago Leytaz (2701m, just under 1h to here).

The path heads essentially E via several hillocks and joins wider Alta Via 4. Yellow arrows point you SSE past several more small lakes with an ample curve to cross a cascading main torrent. At an unmarked junction keep left and down for private Rif. Savoia (2532m). Otherwise the right branch will bring you out at a small lake on the roadside - cut over SE for CAI-run Rif. Città di Chivasso (2604m). (See Walk 19 for information concerning the refuges.)

The actual road pass, Col del Nivolet (2612m, 15 additional min from Rif. Savoia) is slightly uphill from the second refuge.

(Allow 2h30min in ascent.)

RIF. BENEVOLO tel:0165/906143. CAI, sleeps 62 (June weekends, 1/7-20/9)

RIF. CITTÀ DI CHIVASSO tel:0124/953150. CAI, sleeps 30 (end June-20/9)

RIF. ALBERGO SAVOIA tel:0165/94141. Private, sleeps 40 (20/6-20/9)

TOURIST OFFICE BRUIL (Rhêmes-Notre-Dame) tel:0165/96114 (seasonal)

TOURIST OFFICE CERESOLE REALE tel:0124/953121-953186 (seasonal)

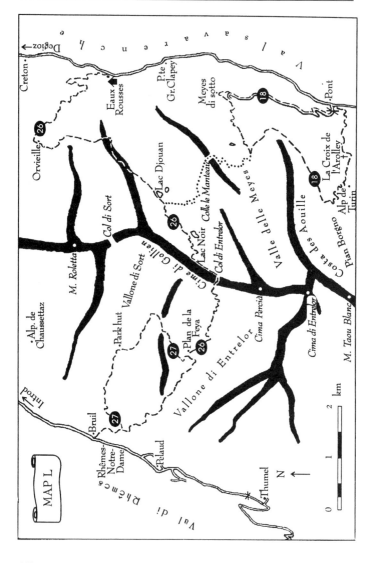

MAP L

WALK 26 *(see map L, p.150)*
Valsavarenche/Val di Rhêmes - Col di Entrelor

via Eaux Rousses - Orvieille (1h30min) - Lac Djouan (1h10min) - Col di Entrelor (1h30min) - Plan de la Feya (1h10min) - Bruil (Rhêmes-Notre-Dame) (1h20min)
Total walking time: **6h40min (1 day)**

Another of the long traverses that make up the Alta Via 2, this one involves some fascinating varied landscapes with stunning views, not to mention wildlife. As there are no intermediate refuges, it is by necessity a 1-day walk. The central section after the 3007m Col di Entrelor is crossed, involves a steep stretch in descent on unstable terrain and is not advisable for beginners early summer as it may be icy. The eastern approach in ascent is however straightforward. The broad valleys on both sides of the pass are well frequented by chamois and ibex, as well as marmots and foxes.

Furthermore both the initial and terminal sections of the itinerary are warmly recommended as easy day trips suitable for families, namely: Eaux Rousses - Orvieille - Lac Djouan and return, as well as the link with the King's Hunting Path in Valle delle Meyes (see Walk 18), and the Plan de la Feya - Vallon di Sort circuit (see Walk 27). *Access:* see Walk 17 for Eaux Rousses, and Walk 24 for Bruil.

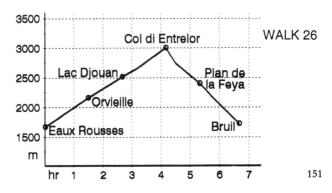

Stage One: ascent via Orvieille (1h30min) and Lac Djouan (1h10min)

Signposted from the main road at Eaux Rousses (1666m) up through the narrow cluster of houses, the route marked regularly for "Laghi" and AV2 turns off the asphalt right behind the Hostellerie du Paradis. Nearby is the trickling waterfall over the rust-coloured rock, stained by the iron in the water that gave the settlement its name. There is a stiff climb N through abandoned terraces and into a dense and beautiful conifer wood mostly of spruce and larch, and home to numerous squirrels and even lone chamois. As well as bilberries, the undergrowth includes the rare twinflower creeper, a delicate pink-white drooping bloom often found on moss cushions.

After about 1h you are joined by a path from the hamlet of Creton (possible alternative access but slightly longer). The wood gives way to pasture and wide curves take you (NW) to the grassy flat of Orvieille (literally "Old Alp", 2164m). The long building belongs to the Park authorities nowadays, but it once hosted royal hunting parties and was a regular site for encampments, even boasting a telegraph line. Views here offer a good range of Valsavarenche peaks, as well as a glimpse of the imposing Gran Combin far away in the N, but the angle widens further with the ascent.

Heading S you follow the fence alongside the buildings where there is drinking water, then climb to a summer farm, where you'll probably have to pick your way through a muddy livestock feeding area. Several more characteristic stone-roofed huts and wooden crosses are passed on dry grassy hillsides infested by carline thistles, crickets and marmots, with swallows overhead. As the trees are left behind, the outlook opens up onto the Gran Paradiso (SE) and surrounding peaks, not to mention the elegant point of the Grivola (NE). Moving SW you gradually enter Vallone dei Laghi, a side valley, its flanks bright red with bilberry shrubs late summer above scattered golden larches. Col di Entrelor is now visible ahead.

The path continues effortlessly to peaceful shallow Lac Djouan (2515m), a perfect picnic spot and worthwhile destination in itself. *Apart from the alpine charr, a type of salmon, and wild ducks, this area is usually rewarding with herds of both chamois and ibex with their young - keep scanning the nearby crests with your binoculars.*

You coast the northern (right) bank of the lake and soon reach a signposted path junction where the Valle delle Meyes link turns off left (S) and can be seen snaking its way up the Costa le Manteau (allow 1h up to Colle le Manteau - see Walk 18).

For Col di Entrelor keep right (SW).

(2h should do in descent to Eaux Rousses from here.)

Stage Two: ascent via Lac Noir (30min) to Col di Entrelor (1h)

The second lake, Lac Noir is actually deep green and lies in a steep-sided basin at 2650m, the silence of which is broken only by tiny twittering ground nesting birds. There are wide curves up the right-hand flank beneath the Cime di Gollien (the name is from the local dialect, and means "small body of water", a reference to the underlying lakes). Among hardy alpine cushion flowers such as saxifrage, the path narrows as the old game track peters out, and a final stretch over loose debris leads to Col di Entrelor (3007m, "between two alps"), N of Cima Percià ("pierced"). From the airy pass, where a spattering of snow is not uncommon, you get a glimpse of M. Blanc (distant NW), then nearby dark grey Becca Tsambellinaz (SW), behind which is Punta Tsantelèynaz ("easy summit") and its glacier in the distance, part of the border with France.

(Allow 1h back down to Lac Djouan.)

Stage Three: descent via Plan de la Feya (1h10min) to Bruil (1h20min)

The path drops steeply W down rough unstable terrain, snow-covered well into summer, though white alpine mouse-ear flowers survive in great numbers. It is both exposed and muddy in parts, but lasts only 20min then you are back onto a decent if narrow path with a more reasonable gradient. This gives you time to appreciate immense desolate Vallone di Entrelor. The small glacier beneath Cima di Entrelor (S) is responsible for the moraine which spills downwards forming long barriers. Ample grassy flats are soon reached with the promise of grazing chamois and romping marmots.

Still keeping to the right-hand side of the valley and in constant descent, you reach the curious vaulted huts of Plan de la Feya (2403m, the name of which means "plain of the sheep"). Pointed Grande Rousse is straight ahead (WNW).

Ignore the yellow waymarking and the path right, and turn decisively left (due W) down a wider path towards the torrent. The first larch trees have appeared, and the right-hand bank of the watercourse is followed to another flowered pasture flat and signpost on a knoll (Entrelor, 2143m, 30min from Plan de la Feya). Several old picturesque buildings are set just off the main path (left), virtually on the edge of this lip of the Val di Rhêmes.

The final 50min consists in a delightful wander essentially NW into a larch wood, golden in late summer with brilliant russet undergrowth, but bilberries for earlier walkers. The path descends in easy zigzags NW, however about halfway down (approx. 1880m) a yellow arrow and the Alta Via marking point off right onto a narrower path. (Should you miss the turning you'll come out at the hamlet of Chaudannaz, only 1.5km by path or road uphill from Bruil.) This leads to an excellent lookout with the unmistakable majestic light limestone form of the Granta Parei at the head of the valley SSW. Diagonally beneath the prominent rock called Château du Couélet (or Castel di Cucco, possibly because it reminded someone of a castle), the path passes huts in a clearing and eventually exits on the valley floor next to the National Park Visitors' Centre (open midsummer only). Across the bridge is the peaceful village of Bruil (1723m, Rhêmes-Notre-Dame). The village has shops, accommodation and a bus stop, not to mention a delightful church where a sun dial reminds passers-by that Nos jours passent comme l'ombre.

(3h45min is necessary in ascent.)

HOSTELLERIE DU PARADIS (Eaux Rousses) tel:0165/905972 Private hotel with a "Foresteria" ie. dormitory. Sleeps 22 (open year-round).
HOTEL GALISIA (Bruil) tel:0165/936100 (open year-round)
TOURIST OFFICE DEGIOZ tel:0165/905816 (seasonal)
TOURIST OFFICE BRUIL (Rhêmes-Notre-Dame) tel:0165/96114 (seasonal)

WALK 27 *(see map L, p.150)*

Val di Rhêmes - Vallone di Sort

via Bruil - Park hut in Vallone di Sort (1h30min) - 2560m saddle (1h) - Plan de la Feya (25min) - Bruil (1h20min)
Total walking time: **4h15min (1 day suggested)**

This loop itinerary climbs one of the lesser-visited side valleys of the Val di Rhêmes, the Vallone di Sort, before traversing an easy saddle to drop into vast and more popular Vallone di Entrelor where the Alta Via 2 itinerary is joined.

Wildlife sightings are virtually guaranteed in all seasons, chamois and marmots in particular, not to mention an excellent range and variety and concentrations of unusual alpine flora.

An alternative round trip route, suitable earlier in the season should late-lying snow block the 2560m pass, heads off N from the Park hut and coasts on n.315 via the Alp. de Chaussettaz (2191m), before a return to Bruil where it comes out at the starting point.

The modest National Park Visitors' Centre at Bruil (open midsummer only) is especially worth a visit for the enormous stuffed exemplary of Lammergeier, or bearded vulture, on display. It is a precious chance to examine this gigantic raptor at close range.

The curious name Rhêmes used for the valley and village groupings prob-ably comes from "remma" or "rame" which means branch or beam in French, a reference to the valley's timber activity.

Access: see Walk 24 for public trans-port. Leave your car in any of the

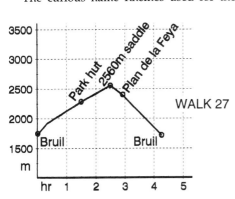

155

ample parking areas at Bruil.

Stage One: via Park hut in Vallone di Sort (1h30min) then 2560m saddle (1h)

From the small square at Bruil (Rhêmes-Notre-Dame, 1723m) take the lane cutting through the old houses and E over the torrent past the National Park Visitors' Centre. A path leads up off the road with AV2 waymarking, and you follow signs for Entrelor/Sort. Past old buildings, some 20min up into the trees, fork off left on n.307, marked for Col du Sort. *The wood is particularly beautiful here, larch mostly but interspersed with Arolla pines and alive with noisy nutcrackers. Underfoot are red cowberries, alpenrose and slender martagon lilies.* The trouble-free path heads due E and climbs into vast silent Vallone di Sort, in the cover of wood all the way to the lovely position of the Park ranger's hut (2285m, drinking water). Scan the nearby ridges S for chamois. The imposing mass of the Grande Rousse (W) dominates the landscape here.

N.307 continues briefly as a wide track SE towards a stream and marmot colonies. In the vicinity of a large wooden pole keep an eye out for the junction right for Vallone di Entrelor. Up now to the ruined huts of Montagna di Sort (2445m). Before turning your back on this upper valley, it's worth a pause to examine the ex-glacial landscape E, as there are some well preserved moraine crests.

A fainter path (SW) climbs over rock marked by the occasional cairn and yellow mark to the ample 2560m saddle that connects the Sort and Entrelor valleys.

(Just over 1h30min for this stage in descent.)

As to views, the Becca Tsambellinaz is SSW, and the Rollettaz NE behind you. Along the crest W from the pass is the Testa di Entrelor (2580m), a somewhat insignificant grassy-rocky knob, but with improved views (30min return).

Stage Two: descent via Plan de la Feya (25min) to Bruil (1h20min)

From the lowest point of the pass cross the grassy slopes in the direction of a small cairn where yellow paint pointers indicate a decisive veer right (SSW). The clear path immediately appears and leads down the side valley to cross a stream. After a stretch left (E) beneath a rock outcrop and old stone walled enclosure, a brief climb

The Grande Rousse seen from the Vallone di Entrelor

brings you out at the barrel-roofed huts of Plan de la Feya (2403m, emergency shelter only).

You have now entered the beautiful Vallone di Entrelor. *This is a haven for sizeable herds of chamois and ibex, either occupying the head of the valley or to be seen grazing or caring for their young on the opposite flanks spread over the vast grassy basins. Wild flowers here come in great quantities, providing spectacular splashes of colour for the impressive backdrop of the Grande Rousse (W), over the Val di Rhêmes.*

The descent path is well trodden and after a series of wide curves down to the level of the torrent keeps to its right bank (see also Walk 26). After a turn-off (30min, optional detour to the Entrelor huts, 2143m) the verge of the valley is reached and must veer right for the descent through another healthy conifer wood. About halfway down (approx. 1880m) a yellow arrow points you right (NW) onto a smaller path. Past a good lookout point for the magnificent Granta Parei SSW, it eventually drops down to the junction in Stage One and returns to Bruil.

(In ascent this stage requires a good 2h30min.)

TOURIST OFFICE BRUIL (Rhêmes-Notre-Dame) tel:0165/96114 (seasonal)

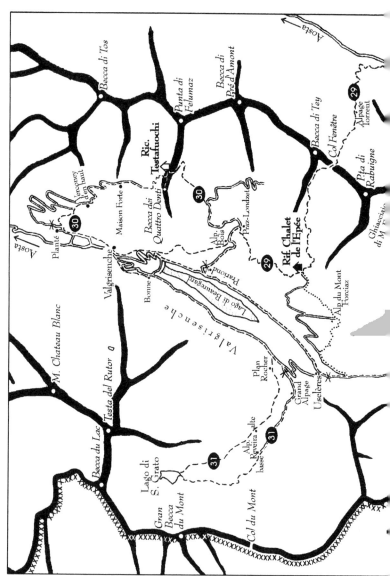

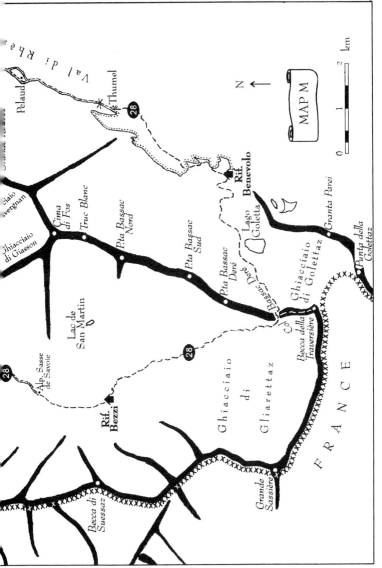

Val di Rhê

Pelaud

Thumel

28

MAP M

N

0 1 2 km

Rif. Benevolo

Ghiacciaio di Giasson

Cima di Fos

Truc Blanc

P.ta Bassac Nord

P.ta Bassac Sud

P.ta Bassac Deré

Lago Goletta

Granta Parei

Bassac Dèré

Ghiacciaio di Golettaz

Punta della Golettaz

Lac de San Martin

Col

Becca della Traversière

Ghiacciaio di Gliarettaz

Alp Sasse de Savoie

28

28

Rif. Bezzi

F R A N C E

Becca di Suessaz

Grande Sassière

WALK 28 *(see map M, p.158/159)*
Val di Rhêmes/Valgrisenche - Becca della Traversière

---

via Bruil - Thumel (1h) - Rif. Benevolo (1h30min) - Lago Goletta (1h30min) - Col Bassac Deré (1h30min) - Becca della Traversière (1h return time) - Rif. Bezzi (2h) - Uselères (1h15min) - Valgrisenche (1h30min)
Total walking time: **11h15min (2-3 days suggested)**

This is a hard walk to beat. Apart from the Thumel-Rif. Benevolo and Uselères-Rif. Bezzi stretches, popular with day walkers due to the magnetism of the refuges, these paths do not see many walkers. Once away from the security of the refuges, you find yourself in wild desolate valleys edged with glaciers, inspiring and sobering.

The optional side trip is quite exceptional - the 3337m Becca della Traversière, part of the Italian-French border, has only recently become accessible for "mere walkers" due to the ongoing retreat of ice on both sides of the Col Bassac Deré pass. A good path leads to a dizzy perch, requiring a good head for heights, with 360° views high above a sea of ice.

Mid to late summer is the best period when snow cover will hopefully be at a manageable minimum, though gaiters are always a good idea. Overall the walk is no more than averagely difficult, and is equally feasible in the opposite direction.

The lower zones described are covered by easy paths, accessible to all ranges of walkers. Rif. Benevolo and Rif. Bezzi, both top scorers on hospitality, make great bases for exploring their respective areas. One of many worthwhile day return trips is Thumel-Rif. Benevolo-Lago Goletta and return, a total of some 5h.
Note: Valgrisenche is both the name for the valley as well as the main village.
Access: see Walk 24 for Bruil.

Valgrisenche has three bus runs a day to and from Aosta, mid-

---

Lago Lillet (Walk 20)

Ascent to Col di Entrelor, with the Grivola - Walk 26
Summit of Punta della Traversière, with the Grande Sassière - Walk 28

WALK 28

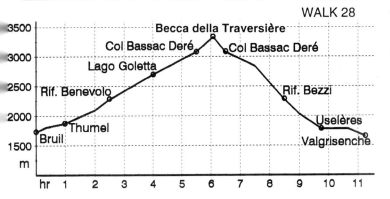

June to the end of September (BENVENUTO company). The rest of the year there are two market runs on Tues, in addition to the buses for the valley's students on Mons and Sats. (The local schools have been closed due to the shrinking population so the valley's children are boarders in Aosta during the week.)

Note: for day trips, you can drive as far as Thumel in Val di Rhêmes, or Uselères via Bonne in Valgrisenche, and thus reduce walking times.

Stage One: ascent via Thumel (1h) to Rif. Benevolo (1h30min)

From the bus stop at Bruil, Rhêmes-Notre-Dame (1723m) leave the village by way of the narrowing surfaced road S. Twenty minutes on is the picturesque hamlet of Pelaud (1811m). Higher up is a large parking area as unauthorised traffic can proceed no further. Some 15min will see you at the active if small farming community of Thumel (1879m).

Where the jeep track curves right (farm and refuge vehicles only - see alt. access), a wide path goes straight ahead SSW. Clearly signposted for Rif. Benevolo, it is also referred to as the "Pison" route, possibly from the name of a local avalanche.

The delightful old paved path follows the right bank of the Dora di Rhêmes torrent most of the way, and is ablaze with unusual flowers such as willow gentians and pink orchids. There are several lovely cascades on the way, and the backdrop is provided by the unmistakable towering Granta Parei massif (S).

At just under 1h from Thumel the path joins the jeep track in the vicinity of a cascade that usually soaks slow passers-by. After the nearby bridge the path cuts up a steep flank, touches on several more buildings and the track again, and clambers up to the natural platform of Rif. Benevolo (2285m).

(Timing in the opposite direction - 2h total.)

Due to its keen managers, experts on the area, this exemplary refuge is brimming with enthusiasm - all manner of information concerning the paths and surroundings is available. As far as facilities go, don't expect more than a spartan wash outside. Drink the tap water at your own discretion, as it has been officially designated as unsuitable for drinking purposes, despite the fact that it comes from a nearby spring. The delicious food however comes in generous portions, and leftovers go to the fox which hangs around in the hope of being fed scraps after dinner.

The Granta Parei lake makes a worthwhile excursion (2h return) from the refuge.

Alternative access via farm track (1h40min)

While only slightly longer, this offers a feasible and more panoramic alternative to the direct path. As the signpost says, it is the access track for Hameau Barmaverein, H. Chantery and H. de Fos, now small summer farms, but once permanently inhabited hamlets. Wide zigzags lead up past the various clusters of old stone houses, complete with a chapel and some interesting vaulted constructions half buried in the mountainside. Marmots abound. The unmistakable shape of the light-coloured Granta Parei can be admired ahead SSW, together with the crown of mountains that close off upper Val di Rhêmes. Keep to the main track at the turn-offs.

Stage Two: climb via Lago Goletta (1h30min) to Col Bassac Deré (1h30min)

In the early morning the Granta Parei, which owes its name to "grande parete" or great wall, is at its best, illuminated to perfection.

From the front of the refuge building, follow the Alta Via 4 triangle waymarking (W) down to the Roman-like stone bridge across the torrent. The easy path climbs diagonally NNW to the old farm buildings of Alp. de Sotses (2313m), then sharp left (S). You pass a turn-off for the Granta Parei lake, and keep right up the steep

Ghiacciaio di Golettaz and recently formed Lago Goletta,
below the Granta Parei

zigzags to the crest where there are magnificent views E to the Gran
Paradiso. This leads SW into the stone desert plateau, Comba di
Golettaz. Ignore a turn-off left for Col Goletta and continue via
guiding cairns along the left bank of the torrent. Below the triangular
point of the Granta Parei (S), the wrinkled surface of the Ghiacciaio
di Golettaz forms the uppermost banks of recently formed grey
Lago Goletta (2699m). An unworldy spot, frequented solely by
enormous grey ravens.

Stepping stones cross the lake's outlet and the path, not always
clear, continues up the right-hand side of the valley. Snow cover
lasts long into the summer in these high reaches, but hopefully
plenty of yellow waymarking will be visible. You climb steadily,
alternating debris and snow. *Surprisingly enough the flora is profuse
midsummer, and the varied colourful rocks, including limestone, host blue*
Mt. Cenis *bellflowers, white alpine mouse-ear and yellow daisies, an
irresistible attraction for butterflies.* The final stretch to the pass crosses
a steep permanent snow field, necessitating a little extra care. You
eventually step out at the narrow saddle of Col Bassac Deré (3082m),
a breathtaking spot. An massive expanse of ice, Ghiacciaio di

Glairettaz, completely fills the next valley, and above it is immense dark Grande Sassière (W). Back E the line-up extends from the Gran Paradiso to the Grivola (NE).

(In descent allow 2h.)

Side trip to Becca della Traversière (1h return time)

This appears to be a well kept local secret in view of the limited numbers of walkers who venture up this far. Under good conditions no actual difficulties are involved, but do remember that on the way down from the peak the path will feel somewhat exposed. Recommended for experienced walkers.

From the pass take the unnumbered path up left (S) and around to a sort of saddle where ibex are possible. A clear path winds up the crest to the giddy top of the Becca della Traversière (3337m), the edge of Italy, where you'll meet mountaineers who've climbed up via rock and ice from the French side. It is simply stunning. Seas of white extend in all directions, and over them with any luck you'll be rewarded by the sight of Mont Blanc (NNW) and the Matterhorn (NW), to mention a few, in addition to the lovely peaks WSW beyond Val d'Isère on the French side.

Take the descent slowly the same way back to Col Bassac Deré.

Stage Three: descent to Rif. Bezzi (2h)

A narrow dirt path (marked Alta Via 4) drops rightish at first to the edge of the glacier, then skirts above it and heads N. The descent is very gradual and problem-free, accompanied by the sight of distant Mont Blanc, not to mention the grandiose ridge to the W. Endless tongues of snow from another reduced glacier are crossed below Punta Bassac Deré then Punta Bassac Sud in a desolate, silent, high altitude landscape, morainic for the most part. *A rainbow of rocks is underfoot, greens, purples and greys, supporting a variety of flora.*

After a good 1h the valley narrows and concertina crevasses on the vast body of ice announce a change of gradient in the form of a sudden drop. The path similarly reaches the edge of an escarpment, still around 2850m, and grassy terrain at last. The refuge is visible below now, while N is the Testa del Rutor, with M. Chateau Blanc slightly right.

The path drops quickly (NNW now), sometimes on loose debris, possibly snow-covered. The thickly flowered terrain is undulating and a couple of side torrents are crossed or forded. Some powerful waterfalls drop from the remnants of glacier on the left.

Welcoming Rif. Bezzi (2284m), set amongst emerald pastures, is eventually reached. *The smaller wing of the hut dates back to the 1930s, but the refuge now boasts a spacious brand new section with all mod cons. Hot showers are available - ask at the bar for a "gettone" token. You're well looked after and well fed here, and the menu features local specialities such as the Valle d'Aosta rice dish "risotto alla valdostana". Half board involves a set menu, many courses long.*

(In ascent allow 2h30min for this stage.)

The refuge can be used as a base for a couple of days while you explore the surroundings: worthwhile trips can be made E of the refuge to Lac de San Martin (2770m, 2h), and for walkers with some climbing experience there is panoramic peak Truc Blanc (3408m, 4h30min).

Stage Four: via Uselères (1h15min) to Valgrisenche (1h30min)

Past the refuge's mechanised cableway, the path (marked for Alta Via 4) heads downhill due N on the right side of the watercourse Dora di Valgrisenche, crossing a side torrent shortly. After 30min the valley opens up considerably and in the vicinity of ruined huts (Alpage Sasse de Savoie, 2036m) overgrown by masses of rosebay willow-herb, a wide motorable track is reached. On the opposite bank are old farm buildings and the start of the cableway.

It's a stroll past several more old farms and down to a track junction - the right fork is for Rif. Chalet de l'Epée (1h45min - see Walk 29 Alternative Access after Stage One). Straight ahead, however, means you shortly reach the abandoned hamlet of Uselères (1785m) and a parking area. *There is also a summer eating place Trattoria Col du Mont, where you can enjoy a tasty meal, snack or just a drink while eavesdropping on the gossip, in the unintelligible dialect-patois of local shepherds.*

The remaining 6-odd km to Valgrisenche mean following the narrow road along above the eastern (right) edge of Lago di Beauregard. *After a good six villages were flooded in the 1950s and this middle section of Valgrisenche destroyed, the dam revealed itself unsafe so had to be drained to the present low maintenance level.* Though the road is surfaced, this stretch is not regularly maintained and is presently in bad condition due to the numerous cascades. This makes it unsuitable for drivers, who should take the newly asphalted road on the opposite bank, but quiet for walkers. At the end of the dam the road curves downwards. Take the path that shortcuts the lower bends (see Walk 30, Stage Two) and emerges at the new sports area, not far from the main centre of Valgrisenche (1664m, bus, shops, hotels).

(In ascent allow about 1h45min from Valgrisenche as far as Uselères, then 2h up to Rif. Bezzi.)

RIF. BENEVOLO tel:0165/906143. CAI, sleeps 62 (June weekends, 1/7-20/9)
RIF. MARIO BEZZI tel:0165/97129. CAI, sleeps 80 (1/7-30/9)
ALBERGO FRASSY (Valgrisenche) tel:0165/97100
TOURIST OFFICE VALGRISENCHE tel:0165/97193 (seasonal)
TOURIST OFFICE BRUIL (Rhêmes-Notre-Dame) tel:0165/96114 (seasonal)

WALK 29 *(see map M, p.158/159)*

Valgrisenche/Val di Rhêmes - The Chalet of Stones

---

via Valgrisenche - Praz-Londzet (2h20min) - Rif. Chalet de l'Epée (45min) - Col Fenêtre (1h20min) - Bruil (2h15min)
Total walking time: **6h40min (1-2 days suggested)**

Another delightful traverse linking quiet rural Valgrisenche with lovely Val di Rhêmes. It lies outside the realms of the National Park, but wildlife is still plentiful. A good path crosses 2840m Col Fenêtre from the west, however snow and ice on the steep eastern side immediately below the pass could be tricky at the very start of the season (the use of an ice pick is sometimes suggested). The itinerary, part of Alta Via 2, has been described west-east here so that the rather long monotonous 1117m ascent is avoided. AV2 walkers

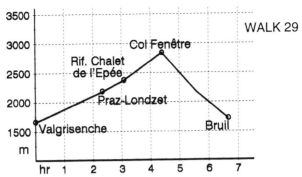

heading the other way will of course have to read it backwards.

The walk lends itself to an excellent variant round trip on the Valgrisenche side, especially suitable for those with a car: park at Uselères, then proceed on the "alternative access" path to Rif. Chalet de l'Epée, traverse to Praz-Londzet, and return via Prariond to Uselères. This will all take some 3h30min.

For notes on the Lago di Beauregard, see Walk 28.

Access: see Walk 28 for Valgrisenche, and Walk 24 for Bruil.

Note: it is possible to drive as far as Uselères for the variant, however take the road via Bonne along the westernmost side of Lago di Beauregard, as the old road on the opposite side is in a very bad state of repair.

Stage One: ascent via Praz-Londzet (2h20min) to Rif. Chalet de l'Epée (45min)

Take the road S out of Valgrisenche (1664m). Not far along, still well below the dam wall near a chapel, signposting for Alta Via 2 points you left across a bridge and around new playing fields. The path intersects the road at times and climbs S through beautiful conifer wood. Some way up, a panoramic rock lookout point provides a good excuse for a rest. Further up, after a stream crossing, the path emerges onto pasture and reaches the picturesque farm building Alp. Bois (2040m).

On a farm access road soon a couple of bends lead E to Praz-Londzet (2180m) and the faded yellow signposted turn-off for Rif. Chalet de l'Epée.

167

SW now the pleasant path climbs easily through larch, alpenrose and bilberries with several brief ups and downs. The final stretch rounds a shoulder beneath Truc de la Seja and you emerge on to the peaceful scenic area to coast along to Rif. Chalet de l'Epée (2370m).

(Allow 2h15min in the opposite direction.)

Its ample outlook ranges over the western flanks of Valgrisenche, where the prominent Rutor peak stands out, with a glimpse of its glacier. The original building, a shepherd's hut, which can be seen in the photo in the restaurant, was called Chalet l'Epère, from "pierres", stones, due to the rocky nature of the surrounding terrain. A comfortable stay is guaranteed in this family-run chalet, opened in summer 1968. Hot showers are available at a modest charge. Meal suggestions include "polenta" (corn meal) mixed with fontina cheese and butter from the nearby family farm, as well as home-made sausages and stews such as "carbonata", in addition to delicious bilberries served with fresh cream. A fitting conclusion is a miniature glass of "grappa" (spirit) flavoured with local aromatic herbs or fruit from the custodian's collection.

Alternative access via Uselères to Rif. Chalet de l'Epée (1h45min)

Just past the abandoned hamlet at Uselères (1785m), park near the modest family-run restaurant Trattoria Col du Mont (warmly recommended for meals).

Take the 4WD track due S for farm and refuge traffic only, from the bend. Some 15min up is a junction with the Rif. Bezzi access track, where you go left (NE) uphill through shady larch trees. Shortly after a set of buildings is passed, take the path that cuts up right (SE), signposted "Rif. Chalet de l'Epée, sentiero panoramico" (whereas continuing via the road takes only 10min more).

You now wind up through a beautiful wood with some magnificent old trees sheltering pale pink alpenrose and concentrations of bilberry shrubs loaded with juicy fruit midsummer. In the openings between, the Gran Becca du Mont appears NW on the border with France, as well as Col du Mont pass (WNW).

One hour will see you in the pasture basin occupied by the Alp. du Mont Forciaz (2180m), beneath the shimmering pocket glaciers of the Grande Rousse SE. Make your way across the marshy terrain and past the buildings. Ignore the yellow arrows up right SSE for Biv. Ravelli, and take the next path up right NNE (wooden sign). It cuts across the dry hillside diagonally and emerges on a rocky basin ablaze with alpenrose. You soon rejoin the vehicle track and pass a modern farm (Alp de l'Epée, 2345m). A little further on is private Rif. Chalet de l'Epée (2370m).

(Just over 1h should suffice in descent as far as Uselères.)

Stage Two: ascent to Col Fenêtre (1h20min)

Head up the signposted livestock track. After a couple of bends you enter another idyllic emerald green pasture valley run through by a meandering stream and inhabited by noisy flocks of yellow-beaked alpine choughs. *The southern side is under light grey scree spills from graceful rock flanks, outrunners of Grande Rousse and home to eagles.* The path keeps to the left-hand side of the stream and runs in the shade of a brownish ridge culminating in the Becca di Tey (E).

The path (well marked) moves easily upwards onto a rock and earth mix with a final wide curve around right (S) to climb to the marker pole at Col Fenêtre (2840m) - don't be tempted by the previous northernmost col. More often than not the pass is presided by ibex, so approach with care as they unfailingly dislodge loose stones if spurred to sudden flight.

This scenic spot includes Gran Becca du Mont WNW, Testa del Rutor NW with Mont Blanc and its group beyond, then facing E you see Gran Paradiso SE, not to mention the village of Bruil some giddy 1100m below on the valley floor.

(1h in descent.)

Stage Three: descent to Bruil, Rhêmes-Notre-Dame (2h15min)

While narrow and steep this path presents no problems for the cautious, in the absence of snow. On incredibly tight zigzags you quickly descend the rubble gully to more stable grassy terrain. A good 20min down, however, on the right-hand side, the path disappears in the midst of fallen rocks and you're better off making your way down the left-hand rubble-strewn side until the path reappears some 100m further down on the right once more.

More zigzags through densely flowered marmot territory continue E.

Approx. 1h10min from the col will see you at some unusual stone huts with broad roofing slabs (Alpage Torrent, 2179m), in symbiosis with the boulders which provide their base. Keeping to the left side of the torrent the earth path descends at a gentler gradient now cutting the steep dry hillsides. *The scene is enlivened by hosts of butterflies such as the red Apollo, common blue and a smaller red and black burnet moth.* Wide curves left around a rock outcrop lead to the temporary shade of larch trees, and the orderly village of Bruil is not far below now amongst manicured patchwork fields.

After a further change of direction (SSW), an unmarked path junction is reached - the right fork descends to fields, a wide agricultural track and eventually joins the asphalt on the edge of peaceful Bruil (1723m). *As well as several sun dials, food shops, a bus stop and a modest hotel, the village boasts a lovely church, reconstructed in the 18th century with an unusual wooden crucifix decorated with a variety of carved objects to symbolise the Passion of Christ. There is also a National Park Visitors' Centre (open summer only) with an astounding stuffed lammergeier, one of the valley's last specimens from the times when the locals were paid to shoot them.*

(3h15min in ascent.)

RIF. CHALET DE L'EPÉE tel:0165/97215. Private, sleeps 60 (20/6-20/9)
HOTEL GALISIA (Rhêmes-Notre-Dame) tel:0165/936100
TOURIST OFFICE VALGRISENCHE tel:0165/97193 (seasonal)
TOURIST OFFICE BRUIL (Rhêmes-Notre-Dame) tel:0165/96114 (seasonal)

WALK 30 *(see map M, p.158/159)*
Valgrisenche - Becca dei Quattro Denti

---

via Valgrisenche - Planté (20min) - Maison Forte (1h40min) - Ric. Testafuochi (1h15mins) - Becca dei Quattro Denti (30min return) - Praz-Londzet (1h15min) - Valgrisenche (1h30min)
Total walking time: **6h30min (1 day suggested)**

While rather lengthy for one day, this marvellous circuit has as its destination the modest 2640m peak, Becca dei Quattro Denti. So

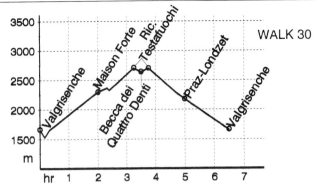

named for the four teeth (quattro denti) of rock along its crest, it is a surprisingly good viewpoint over the multitude of peaks in upper Valgrisenche. An interesting variety of landscapes is covered on the way up, from tranquil conifer woods to thickly flowered meadows and stony slopes. En route are ruins of a historical fort and a series of old stone wall fortifications, which testify to the valley's preparations when faced with an imminent French invasion in the 1790s, the time of Napoleon's Second Italian Campaign.

No difficulties are involved, but a little extra attention is needed for waymarking in several spots. Early walkers should expect some snow cover on the final stretch of ascent to Ric. Testafuochi.
Access: see Walk 28.

It is possible to drive as far as Planté, but this is only useful if a partial walk is planned, as the complete itinerary does not actually return here.

Stage One: via Planté (20min) and Maison Forte (1h40min) to Ric. Testafuochi (1h15min)

From the township of Valgrisenche (1664m), go N down the main road and shortcut through to Gerbelle near the Hotel Grande Sassière, then right and around via Chez Carral. You head towards a yellowish-ochre chapel at the tiny hamlet of Planté (1661m). Soon after the next bend in the road is a faded yellow signpost for the path to Becca dei Quattro Denti. Through fields, the clear path is walled-in at first. At the torrent, keep to the right-hand bank. As the wood starts, the path and yellow arrow waymarking reappear and conduct you up through mixed conifers to a pasture clearing and huts. A brief overgrown stretch and you reach a branch of the dirt track and the abandoned farm Verconey d'en Bas (1825m). SSW upvalley is massive snowcapped Grande Sassière.

The path, marked as n.20 now, heads right (SSE) to the nearby Verconey d'en Haut huts (1980m) and the top of the small ski lift which climbs from Chez Carral (total 50min from Planté).

Follow the recently widened track, and at some old fortifications ignore the yellow/black triangle of an Alta Via 2 variant turn-off right (some 20min up). Stick to the track, which winds up to the low but extensive walls of an old stone fort in ruins, Maison Forte (2295m). *Constructed in 1795 when skirmishes were already regular occurrences between the French and Piedmont soldiers at Col du Mont over to the W, it was a strategic part of the extensive design of Valgrisenche's fortifications.* The position, naturally, means wide-ranging views. The sharp "teeth" of the Becca dei Quattro Denti can be identified up on the ridge S. By all means follow the yellow arrows now, leading past what's left of Alp. Maison Forte, easy to miss. Some 20min on you drop briefly to the edge of the basin directly below the Becca dei Quattro Denti. Keep to its left side on the mule track that makes its way up in countless wide zigzags that give away its military origin.

Snow does tend to accumulate in this area, and should it persist into summer, cut up the slope with care, remembering to keep left. Take the wide gully and head for the slight depression on the crest. (Don't be tempted by the steep narrow zigzags visible up the right - westernmost shoulder of the basin.)

Either way you emerge on the crest at Ric. Testafuochi (2704m) and marvellous views. *The hut is the property of the Forestry Commission, but it is left open and could be useful as emergency shelter (the key is concealed above the innermost door). It is equipped with four bunk beds, a stove of sorts and assorted kitchen utensils, but has no water.* Towering over the next vast pasture amphitheatre, with its old summer farms, is pointed Becca di Tey (SSE), then S is triangular Grande Rousse, while in the opposite direction Testa del Rutor is WNW and M. Chateau Blanc NW.

(Allow 2h in the opposite direction as far as Planté, then 20min to Valgrisenche.)

Side trip to Becca dei Quattro Denti (30min return time)

The actual peak of the Becca dei Quattro Denti, slightly lower in altitude, can be reached by following the narrow crest WSW via a cross and smaller unusable hut, beyond which is the rocky teeth formation, then the 2640m mark. The terrain is crumbly and a sure foot needed.

An alternative descent path for Praz-Londzet drops S from the hut. Though shorter and more direct than the following route, it is narrower and fainter and not suitable for everyone.

Stage Two: descent via Praz-Londzet (1h15min) to Valgrisenche (1h30min)

From Ric. Testafuochi a clear path cuts left (SE) diagonally down the slope amidst extraordinary numbers of pasque flowers. Though it disappears at times, make your way to the stream, below where a clearer route and yellow markers (n.17) appear on the opposite bank. These lead SW alongside the watercourse to a vehicle track (30min so far). Turn right onto it in easy descent. (The alternative path from the crest joins up at the next bend.)

Further down at about 2300m is an old picturesque hamlet in a panoramic position (junction for a variant northwards of Alta Via 2 here). A few more bends through meadows studded with dark purple orchids, and fair-sized Torrente di Praz Londzet is crossed. Not far away now is the signpost and path junction (2180m, usually referred to as Praz-Londzet, not to be confused with the Alpe passed higher up on the road) for Rif. Chalet de l'Epée (see Walk 29).

(In ascent from here, a little over 2h should do.)

Several wide curves of the road in the shade of larch and brightened with flowering alpenrose shrubs lead to a further junction: a signpost points you right across the torrent once more and past another group of typical alpine buildings, Alp. Bois (2040m). A well marked path with yellow and white arrows heads down above a white-washed chapel through meadow, then N across a stream and into the trees. Apart from a brief climb, you descend decisively through a lovely fresh conifer wood, complete with bilberries, via an ample large rocky lookout point. After a brief section of asphalt as you join the road beneath the dam wall, you plunge down again to the lower stream, and across the new playing fields - construction work was under way at the time of writing. Across the bridge to a chapel and signposting, hence the road right for nearby Valgrisenche (1664m, bus, food shop, hotel). (Reverse timing some 2h15mins.)

RICOVERO TESTAFUOCHI Private, sleeps 4 (always open)
HOTEL MAISON DES MYRTILLES (Chez Carral) tel:0165/97118
ALBERGO FRASSY (Valgrisenche) tel:0165/97100
TOURIST OFFICE VALGRISENCHE tel:0165/97193 (seasonal)

WALK 31 *(see map M, p.158/159)*
Valgrisenche - Legendary San Grato

Valgrisenche - Bonne (30min) - Grand Alpage turn-off (1h) - Lago di San Grato (2h15min) - Alp. Reveira alte (45min) - parking area (45min) - Bonne (1h) - Valgrisenche (30min)
Total walking time: **6h45min, or 3h45min with a car (1 day suggested)**

A homage to the intriguing figure of San Grato, 5th century bishop of Aosta and patron saint, combined with an easy pastoral walk in upper Valgrisenche to the lake and chapel named after him. Threatened with persecution in his native Sparta, Grato fled to Rome but through divine messengers learnt that his mission was to evangelise the mountainous area of Aosta. A later vision sent him to the Holy Land for the head of John the Baptist, decapitated by Herod Antipas to reward Salome for her dancing. The ensuing episode is another legend in itself - the miraculous location by an angel of the relic in a deep pit. Back in Rome, when the time came to present the precious trophy to the Pope, only the skull came away leaving the jawbone in the hand of Grato, who carried it back to Aosta, where it is still kept in the Cathedral Treasury in an ornate 15th century reliquary.

The remains of the saint himself are similarly treasured. They were long attributed with miraculous powers, and fragments were in great demand. In the late 14th century they were even stolen, but

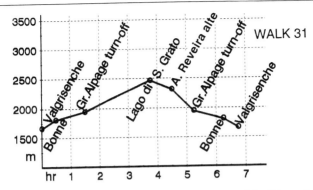

recovered in haste by a determined group of builders from Fontainemore in Valle di Gressoney. During their return journey over alpine passes en route to Aosta, they rested awhile on the shores of what is now known as Lago di San Grato, and a tiny chapel was erected on the spot in remembrance. In modern-day Valgrisenche September 5th is celebrated as "Lo Patron de Sen Grat", and usually involves a procession to the lake and chapel.

Valgrisenche - the name for both the valley and the major settlement - is also well known for its traditional woven woollen fabric, on display at the locally run cooperative workshop where enormous looms are utilised. The unusual "goat battles" (late September) are an added attraction, along with the "Battailles des Reines" with cows.

As far as the walk is concerned, it is rather lengthy if you start out on foot from Valgrisenche. (A highly recommended overnight stay at hospitable Hotel Perret in the upper hamlet of Bonne (1810m) shortens it a little.) While no difficulty is involved in normal conditions, remember that the valley housing the lake tends to accumulate snow which can last well into summer, covering the stream, bridge and path on the upper section. It is therefore more suitable for midsummer, unless you're prepared for snow walking. The return path offers a panoramic alternative to the ascent route, making a ring possible.

Access: see Walk 28.

While the walk description starts from Valgrisenche, drivers can continue via the hamlet of Bonne and SSW along the recently surfaced road to the parking area at the signed turn-off, thus cutting Stages One & Four and some 3h off the total walk time. (**Note:** do not attempt to drive along the opposite side of the lake as the narrow road is in very bad condition.)

Stage One: via Bonne (30min) to Grand Alpage turn-off (1h)

From the bus stop head straight through the small village of Valgrisenche (1664m, food shop). Not far out of the built-up area is the junction right for Bonne. After the open-sided tunnel, a path branches off and proceeds to climb through wood, cutting the road several times. The tranquil hamlet of Bonne (1810m), with its well placed guesthouse, overlooks the dam and Lago di Beauregard. *The lake is deliberately maintained at a low level for safety reasons by the Electricity Commission, due to construction errors. Six villages were "sacrificed" during 1950s flooding in the name of hydroelectricity.*

Follow the road in gradual ascent, coasting S high above the lake. About 1h along, some 4.5km from Bonne, is a signposted turn-off for Lago di San Grato. Drivers should park on the roadside, as the track from here on is restricted to farm vehicles (whereas the road drops to the abandoned hamlet of Uselères).

Stage Two: via Alp. Reveira basse (50min) to Lago di San Grato (1h25min)

Ten minutes will see you at a large old-style summer dairy farm, Grand Alpage (1995m). The wide track continues NW and climbs almost imperceptibly along the northern flank of this ample pasture valley. *Summer is proclaimed by expanses of yellow and white alpine pasque flowers, purple orchids and banks of pink alpenrose shrubs. Romping marmots add the finishing touch.*

High above the torrent stand the long low stone stalls of Alp. Reveira basse (2147m). Here the track narrows soon and just over 5min on, a wooden signpost announces the Lago di San Grato fork to the right. (The main track continues W down to a bridge before innumerable twists and turns in ascent past numerous ex-barracks to the historical 2639m Col du Mont pass and France - a further worthwhile 1h45min. *Long used by the Gauls, the pass also witnessed fighting such as the stand by Piedmont soldiers against the French invasion attempts in the 1790s.*)

As you proceed N up this side valley, Gran Becca du Mont is the peak facing you NW with Becca du Lac due N.

The path soon approaches the gushing torrent near the base of a waterfall, and crosses to the left bank by way of a bridge - if it hasn't been washed away for the nth time.

Alternating gentle climbs and flatter stretches, the path moves up to cut the final steepish flank of this lower basin. As the terrain is unstable and snow often lies late here, expect soft crumbly sections of path, maybe necessitating a few detours.

The minuscule chapel/shrine to San Grato, restored in 1989, stands slightly below Lago di San Grato (2462m) and its grandiose setting. High in the NNE corner of its rocky amphitheatre is Testa del Rutor, on the edge of the massive glacier of the same name which extends northwards (out of sight), while the Becca du Lac dominates in the NNW.

(Allow 1h30min for this stage in the opposite direction.)

Stage Three: return via Alp. Reveira alte (45min) to parking area (45min)
Take the brief narrow concreted passageway across the lake's outlet, and follow the clear path ESE that cuts the steep mountainside, coasting high above the valley you climbed in the last stage. At the faint junctions keep to the lower (right) branch. Gradual descent on this panoramic path leads to Alp. Reveira alte (2318m) about halfway. Wild flowers abound here on this pasture in summer. From this vantage point the eye spaces SE to the graceful line-up of mountains featuring Grande Rousse, then S to the narrow ridge that constitutes the western border of upper Valgrisenche.

Further on at Plan Rocher, cut down to join the road, not far from the parking area. (2h15min should suffice for this stage in the opposite direction.)

Stage Four: return via Bonne (1h) to Valgrisenche (30min)
Take the same route as the access route in Stage One.

HOTEL PERRET (Bonne) tel:0165/97220
ALBERGO FRASSY (Valgrisenche) tel:0165/97100
TOURIST OFFICE VALGRISENCHE tel:0165/97193 (seasonal)

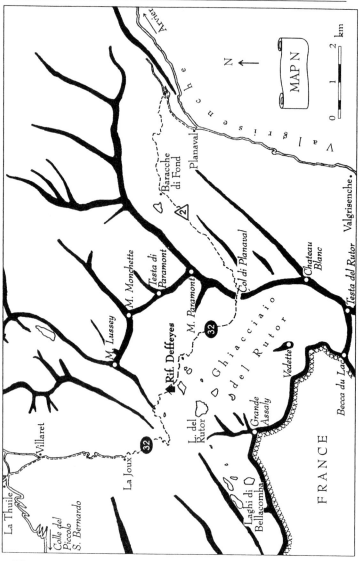

WALK 32 *(see map N, p.178)*
Valle di la Thuile - The Old Man and the Glacier

via La Joux - waterfalls - Rif. Deffeyes (3h) - extension to glacier edge (2h30min return time) - La Joux (2h)
Total walking time: **7h30min (1-2 days suggested)**

Though located several valleys to the west of the National Park, this itinerary is too exciting and rewarding not to be included. A straightforward path via some of the most spectacular waterfalls in the Valle d'Aosta climbs 900m to a hospitable refuge in a breathtaking position - before the vast white expanse of the unusually flat glacier, Ghiacciaio del Rutor (also spelt Ruitor). The name is said to come from local words meaning a rocky point "tor" over a glacier, however another version links it to the Latin "rivus torsus", tortuous stream, originally used for the watercourse that ran through La Thuile. This locality on the other hand, called Ariolica under the Romans, owes its name either to a French version of "Tegula", the stone slabs long used here for roofing, or from Tullius Cicero, Caesar's lieutenant in the glorious 54-52 BC war against the Gauls.

An excellent winter resort thanks to its proximity and links to the French ski fields of La Rosière and Colle del Piccolo San Bernardo, La Thuile needs no introduction to English skiers.

While the complete walk can be done in a day at a pinch, it is a pity to rush, and an overnight stay at Rif. Deffeyes is warmly recommended. Furthermore a pleasant day could be profitably spent exploring the surroundings, including the extension described. High altitude alpine flora and marmots are guaranteed, not to mention a variety of glacier-related phenomena.

A shorter day variant could go as far as any of the waterfalls - 2h30min return time for the third fall. Another recommended walk in this area is to the Laghi di Bellacomba, a series of lakes in a beautiful and solitary elongated valley. It is a straightforward route from the junction in Stage Two (allow 5h return time from La Joux).

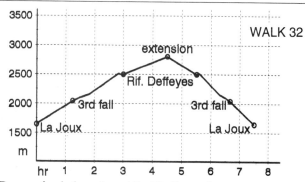

Do any food shopping at La Thuile as there are no facilities further on.

Access: La Thuile is served by year-round bus (SAVDA) from the railway station at Pré-St-Didier in Valle d'Aosta. For La Joux, the summer line (run by La Thuile council) is limited to the central 2-3 weeks of August. **Drivers note:** the 4km road to La Joux is rather narrow on the last stretch in ascent, and access may be restricted at peak times.

On foot from La Thuile (1447m) take the road past the tourist office signposted for La Joux and "cascate". Keep straight on (S) at all the junctions. After the bridge, where the road narrows and starts climbing, are plenty of shortcuts. 1h will do (45min in descent).

Stage One: La Joux to the first (15min), second and third falls (1h)
La Joux (1650m) is essentially a scattering of modest summer restaurants and pasture. Before starting you'll notice a prominent triangular-shaped peak due S - the Grande Assaly will come in and out of view on countless occasions, before appearing in all its glory up on the level of the refuge.

Not far from the bus stop and limited parking area, clear signposting, including the yellow and black markings of the Alta Via 2, indicates the popular path off left for the waterfalls. Over a bridge, it climbs easily S, never far from the rushing water. *The cool wood of mixed conifer has undergrowth of pink flowering alpenrose.* Fifteen minutes are enough for the ample viewing area for the "1ª (prima) cascata" - first fall.

The third fall en route to Rif. Deffeyes

In steady ascent through smooth rock passages, past an old hut (Parlet, 1774m), you reach a raspberry-rich clearing. A rickety bridge turn-off to the right is passed (an interesting alternative - some 30min to a panoramic viewing point for the top two waterfalls and their combined 300m drop). You coast alongside the stream for a while. Becoming steeper, the path approaches the brief detour to the base of the second fall - signposted as the "2ª (seconda) cascata".

Back on the main path in the wood, predominantly larch and Arolla pines here due to the higher altitude, the path continues upwards to a similar detour for the base of the upper and final fall - the "3ª (terza) cascata", also the most dramatic. As volumes of glacial water thunder down the ancient rock channel, sprays of suspended mist are whipped over unsuspecting visitors by the lightest breeze. Daring shrubs cling to overhanging holds. *(Total 1h15min this far.)*

Stage Two: continuation to Rif. Deffeyes (1h45min)
As you proceed unrelentingly upwards, the landscape undergoes a dramatic change as you emerge from the wood. Not long afterwards you pass the signed turn-off (15min from the last fall) for the Laghi di Bellacomba (2374m, allow at least 1h40min from here). The path heads leftish (E) away from the watercourse, via a rock corridor where marmots play hide and seek among late summer's reddening bilberry shrubs. The outlook, including ample views W and N to La Thuile and beyond, opens up considerably. An unusual elongated valley follows, flat-bottomed due to the accumulated silt and now housing Lac du Glacier. Left across the bridge are the modest buildings of Alpage du Glacier (2158m, 20min from the turn-off). Ample curves past the rare lone Arolla pine lead up the northernmost flank of the basin, the remains of an old mechanised cableway nearby. Once the edge of the wide crest has been attained, it's hard to know where to look: back NNW Mont Blanc stands out clearly, whereas ahead are the first glimpses of the unbelievable spread of Ghiacciaio del Rutor, whose horizon features the unusual wedge shape of the Vedette (SSE). Once you're through the wide passage, the wooden-shuttered refuge building comes into sight. The old shepherds' huts nearby are occasionally used for supplementary accommodation.

Rif. Deffeyes (2494m), named after a fervent supporter of the Valle d'Aosta ethnic and linguistic minority, is run by a helpful custodian aided by an amiable and creative cook whose mouth-watering dishes have become famous. The position, of course, is simply magnificent.

The Grande Assaly is now a distinct and impressive knife blade SSW, whereas SSE over the glacier is the Testa del Rutor, quite insignificant from this angle. M. Paramont is due E.

The inconspicuous solar panels below the main building power the anaerobic treatment plant for both liquid and solid waste. The main tanks are out of sight underground, and make use of European Union funding and state-of-the-art technology.

Nowadays the front of Ghiacciaio del Rutor measures some 3km in length. Once, much more extensive, its barrier often collapsed under the pressure of water and ice and caused dramatic floods in the valleys below. One such event was recorded in 1680 causing widespread damage, even as far away as Villeneuve in Valle d'Aosta, where the bridge was destroyed. In alternative to the costly proposal to bore drainage channels through the mountain sides, processions bearing the head of San Grato became a regular event. That all came to an end in the late 19th century when the climate warmed somewhat, marking the end of a mini-ice age. As the ice sheet retreated, it left extensive hollows where several lakes formed, and they now colour the long valley or "comba" below the refuge with their turquoise tinges.

Alongside the scientific accounts is an age-old legend that says the area now under ice was once rich pasture. One day, the story goes, Christ was on earth to see what use man had made of the gifts bestowed on him by God. Disguised as a beggar he asked for a drink of milk, to which a rude shepherd retorted that he would rather pour his milk away than waste a drop on an old tramp such as he. This he subsequently did, overturning a large pail, the milk draining away in white streams. His iniquity incurred the wrath of God and those white streams continued to gush and spout from the earth itself. The consequent enormous blocks of ice formed a terrible wave of destruction which completely submerged the area, inhabitants included. Only a young mother and her child managed to escape. The old shepherd himself lives on beneath the ice in his milky tomb, his rage the cause of the creaking and sudden movements of the glacier. As he cries with frustration at his impotence, his tears flow out from beneath the ice to form the lakes, streams and waterfalls lower down. The bitter taste of the water comes from his soul, and the icy cold his heart. No wonder it is undrinkable!

Stage Three: extension to upper glacier edge (2h30min return time)

The AV2 path leads high above the northeastern edge of the ice mass with some more marvellous views, and can be profitably followed for a good way before it actually moves onto the glacier.

From the refuge take the path straight down over the torrent. A gradual climb leads ESE around countless picturesque lakes in sheltered pockets, the refuge out of sight. *Clusters of glacially smoothed rocks, roches moutonnées, pretty alpine blooms and whistling marmots are frequent, but the ever improving outlook over the expanse of ice tends to dominate the attention.*

The path winds its way through rock-earth terrain, its regular yellow arrow waymarking supplemented by small heaps of stones, cairns. A stretch due S leads to a breathtaking ridge where the gaze spaces out over the glacier, wrinkled with narrow but deep longitudinal crevasses, and its surface corrugated in the absence of snow. It is, however, equally famous for the unexpected thick mists that roll over it.

From the belvedere, the path drops somewhat bearing E, to coast above the glacier edge and a tiny grey lake. A slowish climb SE takes you to an old moraine ridge, at the foot of a rock wall. Here (approx. 2800m) the route drops down right onto the glacier itself and can only be followed by those suitably experienced and equipped with crampons and ice pick (it proceeds to Col di Planaval hence Planaval in Valgrisenche). "Mere walkers" will have to be content with this breathtaking scenario, which includes a clear view now of the prominent Testa del Rutor SSE.

Stage Four: return to La Joux (2h)

From the refuge the return route to La Joux is the same as that taken in ascent.

RIF. E. DEFFEYES tel:0165/884239 CAI, sleeps 80 (25/6-20/9)
HOTEL CHALET ALPINA (La Thuile) tel:0165/884187 (English speakers)
TOURIST OFFICE LA THUILE tel:0165/884179

APPENDICES

Alta Via 2

Long fatiguing climbs to airy passes as high as 3300m, each with the reward of a superb new sweep of ice and snowbound summits. Walkers are plunged into wild valleys where close encounters with the myriad animal life become daily affairs. This long-distance route through the Gran Paradiso National Park connects the eastern edge of Valle d'Aosta with its western extreme, Val Veny, at the foot of the Mont Blanc massif. At a pinch, fit walkers could complete the Alta Via 2 in seven days. However a recommended approach is to spend at least one day off the main route at each overnight stop to explore the higher reaches of each valley encountered.

Mindful of the long climbs and descents involved in each stage, it is definitely feasible for average walkers with the notable exception of the Col di Planaval passage. This involves a brief glacier traverse necessitating experience and suitable equipment (crampons and ice pick minimum). It can, however, easily be detoured by a series of bus connections to the next valley and La Thuile, and resumed from there.

The route diagrams show the complete route in summary form, including references to the relevant Walk descriptions and extra notes for other sections. While timing is given for both directions, east-west is recommended - this ensures a rewarding conclusion with the emotion of the magnificent sight of the Mont Blanc massif with its glaciers pouring into Val Veny.

The Valle d'Aosta Regional Authority has produced a useful brochure on the Alta Via 2 (in combination with the Alta Via 1 on its northern side). It contains map sections and some practical details, long out-of-date in many cases, and is available from the helpful Aosta Tourist Office, Piazza Chanoux 8, 11100 Aosta (tel:0165/23667).

The complete AV2 route is covered by the 1:50,000 walking maps by IGC n.3 (Il Parco Nazionale del Gran Paradiso) or FMB's "Gran Paradiso", with the addition of IGC sheet n.4 or the FMB "Monte Bianco" for the La Thuile-Courmayeur part.

Alta Via ②

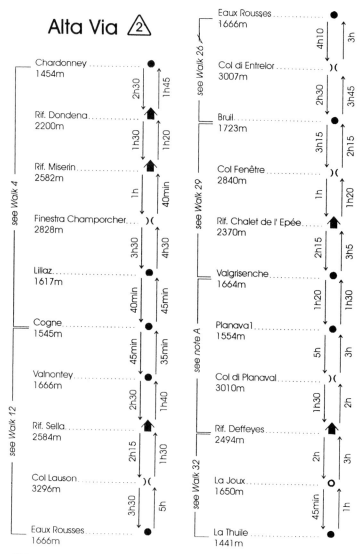

Chardonney 1454m

2h30 / 1h45

Rif. Dondena 2200m

1h30 / 1h20

Rif. Miserin 2582m

1h / 40min

Finestra Champorcher 2828m

3h30 / 4h30

Lillaz 1617m

40min / 45min

Cogne 1545m

45min / 35min

Valnontey 1666m

2h30 / 1h40

Rif. Sella 2584m

2h15 / 1h30

Col Lauson 3296m

3h30 / 5h

Eaux Rousses 1666m

see Walk 4

see Walk 12

Eaux Rousses 1666m

4h10 / 3h

Col di Entrelor 3007m

2h30 / 3h45

Bruil 1723m

3h15 / 2h15

Col Fenêtre 2840m

1h / 1h20

Rif. Chalet de l' Epée 2370m

2h15 / 3h5

Valgrisenche 1664m

1h20 / 1h30

Planaval 1554m

5h / 3h

Col di Planaval 3010m

1h30 / 2h

Rif. Deffeyes 2494m

2h / 3h

La Joux 1650m

45min / 1h

La Thuile 1441m

see Walk 26

see Walk 29

see note A

see Walk 32

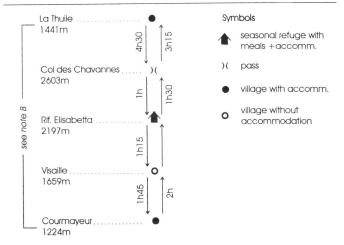

Special AV2 waymarking consists of a yellow triangle containing a "2", as well as yellow arrows. It is supplemented by signposting at key points, giving intermediate timing and altitudes, however most are so faded nowadays as to be useless except as reference points.

Apart from the refuges, accommodation is in valley guesthouses, for which advance reservation is advisable in midsummer. Camping is feasible if you're used to carrying the extra weight. Do remember that the National Park does not allow wild pitches within its borders.

The following notes refer to the route diagram.

Note A: Valgrisenche - Planaval - Col di Planaval - Rif. Deffeyes
(see map N, p.178)
Note: Glacier crossing involved - experienced and equipped walkers only.

For the 6km between the village of Valgrisenche and Planaval, AV2 follows the road (occasional bus), turning off the main road for the final 10min to the modest guesthouse *(Hotel Paramont tel:0165/97106)*.

From here, after 20min of surfaced farm track NE amongst masses of wild roses, AV2 heads E to climb into a tranquil pasture

187

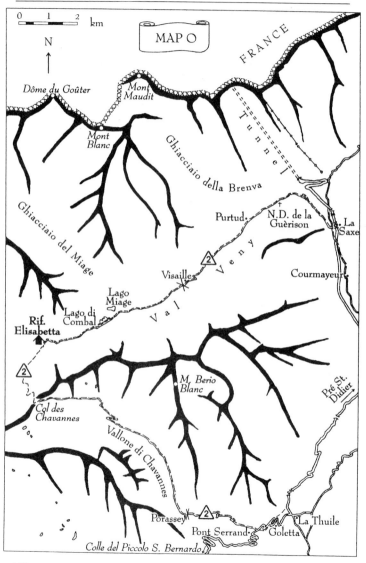

MAP O

valley alongside a picturesque gurgling watercourse. Following a group of ruined huts (Baracche di Fondo, 2340m, 2h10min) you cross to the left-hand side of the stream. The climb continues, with waymarking uncertain at times, to moraine crests before actually moving onto Ghiacciaio del Rutor. Crevasses may be encountered on the final stretch to renowned panoramic Col di Planaval. In descent, some 30min bearing right will see you on a moraine crest. For the final easy 1h to Rif. Deffeyes, see the extension in Walk 32.

Note B: La Thuile - Col des Chavannes - Rif. Elisabetta - Visaille - Courmayeur (see map O, p.188)

This section is problem-free, if rather long. AV2 leaves La Thuile briefly downhill from the bus stop. Once across the torrent the old road climbs SW and cuts the wide curves of the Colle del Piccolo San Bernardo road. Some 30min up just before Pont Serrand, the route turns off right (W) onto a rather monotonous narrow asphalt road past several dairy farms and ending at Porassey (1900m, 1h45min this far). A wide dirt track leads N through the narrow entrance of long treeless but thickly flowered pasture valley, Vallone di Chavannes. *The valley owes its name to a specialised late Latin name for kitchen premises adjoining a summer farm!* Climbing gradually as it veers W, the path offers stunning views back to Ghiacciaio del Rutor SE. Keep right at the main track turn-off. Col des Chavannes, where snow is possible early summer, merits a slow approach, as the ensuing outlook over the Val Veny onto the Mont Blanc group is simply breathtaking.

From the pass a narrow path drops diagonally (N) down a mobile detritus slope which may require a little care. 15min though and you'll be on easy grass terrain, all the way down to the valley floor, once the site of a Roman road. It's not far NE now to *Rif. Elisabetta Soldini (CAI, tel:0165/844080, sleeps 80, 15/6-15/9)*, close to the immense ice drop from the Ghiacciaio de la Lex Blanche.

Continuing down the 4WD track, the next noteworthy feature after marsh-like Lago di Combal is hidden behind the intriguing wall of debris-cum-moraine of the Ghiacciaio del Miage which all but bars the valley. The 30min detour to Lago Miage is compulsory: a milky-grey lake flanked by a towering wall of ice which continues to topple trees in its path.

A steep surfaced road, recently closed to traffic due to colossal landslides, quickly leads to Visaille and its bar-restaurant. The summer (1/7-10/9) bus to Courmayeur starts from here, as does another fascinating side trip (2h30min return time) to the Giardino del Miage, a pocket garden oasis of larch entrapped between the arms of the advancing glacier.

There are several camping grounds and two hotels *(3-star Purtud, tel:0165/869084; 2-star Val Veny tel:0165/868717)*, but though they open late June-July, everything unfortunately closes down early September the minute the Italian school year starts.

Despite the tourist traffic, even on foot this final asphalted section has many distractions for the footsore, starting with the spectacular Ghiacciaio della Brenva which crashes valleywards from Mont Blanc. The last leg of the itinerary passes the chapel of Notre Dame de la Guèrison. *The chapel is an impassable barrier for the multitude of devils and witches banished to the valley's high icy realms, as well as providing hope for young women in search of a husband.* Then down the mountainside through La Saxe to the rather pricey resort of Courmayeur, where you can collapse in a wide range of accommodation *(Tourist Office tel:0165/842060)*.

Typical "Alta Via 2" waymarking

GLOSSARY

acqua (non) potabile	water (not) suitable for drinking
agibile (inagibile)	usable and consequently accessible and open (unusable hence closed), referring to a hut, path etc.
aiuto!	help!
alpage, alpe	summer pasture area and/or hut
alta via	long distance high level route
alto	high
altopiano, altipiano	high altitude plateau
balma	originally a reference to the space beneath rock overhangs or erratic blocks traditionally used as shelter by herdsmen, later transformed into primitive dwellings with dry stone walls
becca, cima, punta, testa	mountain peak, summit
bivacco	bivouac hut, unmanned
bocca, bocchetta, col, colle, finestra, fenêtre, passo	mountain pass
borgata, frazione, hameau	hamlet
caduta sassi	falling rocks
camere libere	rooms free
capanna, casotto	hut
capoluogo	provincial or regional capital, or township
cascata	waterfall
cengia	ledge
comba, combe	long narrow valley
costa	flank, slope
cresta	crest, ridge
diga	dam
est/orientale	east/eastern
facile	easy
fiume	river
funivia	cable-car
ghiacciaio	glacier
grangia	stone hut in pasture zone, used seasonally for men and livestock
lac (lacs), lago (laghi)	lake (lakes)
località	place, locality
mayen	a medium-altitude farm that can be utilised early (such as May, hence the name) to provide livestock with fresh grass
montagna	high altitude summer farm (Valle d'Aosta)
muanda	high altitude summer farm (Piedmont)
nord/settentrionale	north/northern
ovest/occidentale	west/western
palestra di roccia	rock-climbing area, often with marked routes

pedonale	for pedestrians
pericolo/pericoloso	danger/dangerous
piano	plain, plateau on maps (cf. slowly or quietly as an instruction)
ponte	bridge
posto tappa	a village building adapted to provide basic accommodation for walkers
ricovero	literally shelter, such as an ex-military hut, but unless adapted as bivouac hut, usually abandoned
ricovero invernale	winter quarters adjoining a refuge
rifugio	mountain hut or inn, usually manned
rio, torrente	mountain stream
san, santo, santa	saint
seggiovia	chair lift
sentiero	path
soccorso alpino	mountain rescue
sorgente	spring (water)
sud/meridionale	south/southern
telecabina	type of cable-car
tornante	hairpin bend
torre	tower
val, valle, vallon, vallone	valley

REFERENCES

Andreis E., Chabod R. & Santi M.C. (1980) *Gran Paradiso, Parco Nazionale* Guida dei Monti d'Italia, CAI/TCI, Milano.

Balliano A. (1951) *Aria di leggende in Val d'Aosta* Cappelli, Bologna.

Bersezio L. & Tirone P. (1988) *Andar per Rifugi* Istituto Geografico De Agostini, Novara.

Buffo G. (1995) *Curiosità, misteri e leggende del Piemonte e della Valle d'Aosta* Tipografia Ferraro - Editrice in Ivrea.

Chiaretta F. (1995) "La Forza dell'Orco. Tra i laghi artificiali del Paradiso". *ALP*, n.125, Torino.

Gatto Chanu T. (1991) *Leggende e racconti della Valle d'Aosta* Newton Compton Editori, Roma.

Giorgetta A. (1985) *Alpi Graie Centrali* Guida dei Monti d'Italia, CAI/TCI, Milano.

Mari A. & Kindl U. (1988) *La montagna e le sue leggende* Mondadori, Milano.

Various Authors (1992) *Il Parco Nazionale Gran Paradiso* Kosmos Edizioni, Torino.

Various Authors (1991) *Valle d'Aosta* Istituto Geografico De Agostini, Novara.

Yeld G. & Coolidge W.A.B. (1893) *The Mountains of Cogne* T. Fisher Unwin, London.

Brochures and maps kindly provided by local Tourist Offices, in addition to the Park Authority's newsletter.

PRINTED BY
CARNMOR PRINT & DESIGN, LONDON ROAD, PRESTON. UK